DOMINIC BARBERI

Father Dominic Barberi, CP
A drawing from life by 'Dicky' Doyle

DOMINIC BARBERI

GERARD SKINNER

GRACEWING

First published in England in 2021
by
Gracewing
2 Southern Avenue
Leominster
Herefordshire HR6 0QF
United Kingdom
www.gracewing.co.uk

The publishers have no responsibility for the
persistence or accuracy of URLs for websites referred
to in this publication, and do not guarantee that any
content on such websites is, or will remain, accurate
or appropriate.

ISBN 978 085244 977 6

Cover design by Bernardita Peña Hurtado

Typeset by Word and Page, Chester, UK

CONTENTS

For my father

INTRODUCTION & ACKNOWLEDGEMENTS

Most biographies of Newman pass over the name of Blessed Dominic Barberi with hardly a sideways glance, yet St John Henry Newman himself saw Blessed Dominic's part in his conversion as much more than merely incidental.

This is but a short and simple introduction to the life of Blessed Dominic Barberi, largely drawn from a much longer biography published in 1967 by the Passionist Alfred Wilson entitled *Blessed Dominic Barberi—Supernaturalized Briton*. Wilson, in his turn, drew material from previously published works, above all from biographies by Passionists who knew Blessed Dominic himself. More recently, in 2008, the indefatigable Fr Ben Lodge published a very readable account of Blessed Dominic's life as part of a *Catholic Truth Society* series, 'Saints of the Isles'. A truly magisterial biography of the Beatus is, however, a very long way off due to the fact that so many of the books that he wrote and other texts over which he laboured have not yet been transcribed from his almost illegible handwriting.

I am grateful to the Rev'd Ben Lodge, CP, the Rev'd Paul Francis Spencer, CP, the General Archives of the Passionists (Rome), the Rev'd Paul Keane and Professor Maurice Whitehead for their assistance in writing this short biography.

Early Years

SUCH KNOWLEDGE AS WE HAVE about the early life of Dominic Barberi emerges from registers, his written recollections and the memories of others of the stories he told. He was born on 22 June 1792 some fifty miles north of Rome in the little hamlet of Palanzana, near Viterbo, to Giuseppe and Maria Barberi. Two days later he was baptised in the Church of St John the Baptist, being given the names Dominic John Aloysius. His parents were devout tenant-farmers, Dominic being the youngest of eleven children.

Giuseppe Barberi died on 26 March 1798, leaving Dominic with hazy impressions of him but clear memories of his mother. It was she who taught Dominic by word and example. From her he imbued a joyful, trusting spirit, a compassionate care for others and an aptitude for hard work. Whilst her trust in the providence of God was absolute, this did not hinder her in seeing the role of the will in difficult situations: 'a hundred years of gloom do not pay off a farthing of debt' was among her sayings later recalled by Dominic. When her children misbehaved, she would say 'children you can be saints!' The future Beatus admitted that 'as a child I experienced great difficulty in submitting to my parents'.[1]

The charity of his mother was well known to the family's neighbours, Maria Barberi frequently giving away food to those she felt were in greater need than her own family. Barberi's mother never tired of reminding her children that the Blessed Virgin Mary, their heavenly mother, loved them so much more than she was able to. Her devotion was, in Dominic's heart, given real authority when a Capuchin priest asked the young Dominic, 'Son are you fond of the Madonna? The Madonna, you know, loves you much more than your mother.' Dominic later wrote, 'These words struck me so forcibly that I often reflected on them as I was going about, and whenever my mother made a fuss of me, the thought came to my mind that the Madonna loved me even more than she'.[2] Dominic's mother taught her children to fast every Saturday and on the vigils of solemn Marian feasts.[3]

The total trust of Maria Barberi in her patron saint left an indelible impression on Dominic. Among many instances of his mother's trust in Our Lady he recalled how, after falling off her donkey and breaking her arm, she was told that she would have to remain in hospital for a month and so immediately entrusted herself to the Blessed Virgin Mary by saying the Rosary. When she fell asleep, she dreamt that she felt a soft hand gently stroking her broken arm. Upon awakening she was convinced that she was cured and asked the astonished nurse to remove her bandages. Her arm was indeed strong again and she returned home to look after her family as she had hoped.[4]

A further instance from his early years confirms the spiritual life of the Barberi family. Tragically and totally unexpectedly Dominic saw his favourite sister, the ten-year-old Rosa, collapse and die. His mother was not at home at the time and as she approached the house Dominic ran out exclaiming, 'Mamma, Rosa is dead'. Too young to understand, Dominic was surprised at his mother's horrified reaction, asking her 'Why, Mamma, isn't Rosa lucky to have gone to heaven so soon?'[5]

That was not the reaction of Dominic after the death of his mother on 23 March 1803. It seems that she had a presentiment that was soon to die, even sewing together her own shroud in preparation for burial. Dominic was distraught at her passing, but his mother's strong faith was growing in him:

> That day you inspired me with greater confidence than ever in your maternal protection. I recall — how vividly I recall! — that day when I was orphaned and felt like one derelict and abandoned in an unknown continent. I had recourse to you, and only dimly aware of what I said, exclaimed, 'O! Most holy Virgin you see my plight. You see that I am deprived of a mother on earth, so now it is up to you to be my Mother. To you I commit myself, in you I trust, from today you shall be my Mother.'[6]

Although his mother knew that Dominic was an intelligent child, she still believed that formal schooling was unnecessary. This did not prevent Dominic from asking to be allowed to study. He had occasional lessons with the Capuchins of Palanzana from whom he received a grounding in grammar as well as spiritual guidance. They, and Maria Barberi, encouraged Dominic to become a Friar, but Dominic was not so inclined.

Whatever his education, Dominic certainly learned to read and clearly had a prodigious memory, memorizing whole tracts of scripture and, in later life, poetry and canon law as well. But his learning was deeper than mere parrot-fashion recall, he also learnt to hear the voice of God in prayer:

> I recall, my God, that almost as soon as I came to the use of reason You made Yourself known to me in a mysterious way. Exciting alluring attractions for you in my heart, You permitted me to hear You whispering in my ear 'Love Me, my son'. How satisfying were the attractions which I experienced when You deigned to draw me to You as I was engaged in my exercises of piety and religion.[7]

Dominic was confirmed at the age of seven in the Bishop of Viterbo's chapel, receiving his First Holy Communion five years later, as was the practice at the time. He recited the rosary daily and frequented the Sacraments.

Youth

W ITH THE DEATH OF HIS MOTHER, the Barberi children were entrusted to different members of the extended family, Dominic given into the care of his maternal uncle, Bartholomew Paccelli, and his wife Cecilia who lived in Merlano, a village not so very far from Palanzana. The Pacellis loved Dominic as if he were their own but, whilst ensuring that he was materially well provided for, they, like Maria Barberi, in no way thought that their new charge could benefit from school. Whether or not they indulged Dominic, perhaps out of sorrow for the undoubted distress that he had endured having lost both his parents and being separated from his siblings, is open to question. In later life Fr Dominic wrote, at the instruction of his spiritual director, an autobiography entitled *Outline of the Divine Mercy in the Conversion of a Sinner*. From this source accounts of his teenage years have been written. In the autobiography he reflects on the results of his indiscriminate reading at this time—a time which was heavily coloured by the thinking that had inspired the French revolution. Dominic continued to frequent the sacraments and say his prayers yet, he wrote,

> Piety seemed to me despicable, and the only men worth calling great, those who had enlightened the world by arms or literary work. I considered the Christian religion mean and contemptible, and the world debased by having become Christian. I berated the Emperor Constantine for having forced the Romans to embrace Christianity.[8]

And then Dominic fell in love. But the girl in question was already engaged. She married and Dominic's response was to celebrate by singing the Church's great hymn of praise, the *Te Deum*. In his heart of hearts, he knew that his true happiness lay elsewhere.

It was at this time that Dominic first made the acquaintance of the order that one day he was to join. Following Napoleon's suppression of religious communities, members of the Passionists, among many other orders, found themselves dispersed and needing shelter. Four Passionists—Frs Paolo Luigi, Gioacchino, Giuseppe and Br Giorgio of the Resurrection came to live in the neighbourhood where Dominic was living. The Passionists had been founded in Italy by St Paul of the Cross (1694–1775) as a missionary order. Their Rule was strict and austere—grounded in hours of solitary meditation upon the Passion of Christ, each Passionist was then to go out into the world giving missions and retreats.

Dominic was delighted to find that the Passionists had brought their library with them and so he set about immersing himself amongst the volumes that he found there having served Mass for them each day in their chapel. He found himself strangely moved by the insignia that the Passionists wore on their chests—the heart surmounted by the Cross— and the Passionists themselves were impressed by Dominic's lively interest thus one was happy to give him lessons in Italian and another lessons in French, a much hated but useful language in view of the French soldiers who were now in charge of the country.

To some extent, Dominic's religious zeal revived, but not to such an extent as he was able to withstand the temptation to what he later recalled as improper conversation which he confessed to one of the Passionists. The Father was kind but stern. But Dominic relates that when he confessed the same sin again to the same priest, probably admitting that he had not really attempted to amend his ways the first time, the priest refused him absolution. He was informed that he had to reform his life for a fixed period of time before he might be granted absolution. Dominic's autobiography records,

> This blow, reinforced by divine grace, gave me such a shock that, for a time, I was beside myself. Despite my hardness of heart, I went to the Church, and there, before a statue of Our Lady, began to bewail my misfortune. 'Poor me,' I cried, 'if I died now, what would become of me? I am excluded from Holy Communion and unworthy to receive my God! And to think that I should have come to this pass for the sake

of fatuous and fruitless conversations! Lord help me, I don't want to do this again.' I then conceived such intense sorrow for my sins that the mere remembrance of them filled me with horror. I felt classed with the excommunicated and cut off from the body of the faithful.[9]

Dominic reflected on his confessor's reproof: 'How true is the saying of Bellarmine that there would not be such great facility in sinning if there were not such great facility in absolving.'[10] However, in later life he was strongly critical of

Indiscreet confessors who drive penitents from them because they are unable to break bad habits all at once. How opportune would be a little more patience! When I meet impatient confessors, I say to myself: it is evident that this confessor has never been a sinner himself. If he had been a sinner himself, he would have a little more sympathy for these unfortunates.[11]

After having completed his 'probation' an undoubtedly nervous Dominic Barberi returned to the confessional. A different, and kinder, confessor awaited him, giving him for his penance the instruction to make a quarter of an hour's mental prayer every day. This was a novelty for him, and he had to ask the priest what mental prayer was and how he should go about practicing it. And so

Before going to bed—I have always found this time most helpful for this exercise—I recommended myself to the Madonna and begged for her help; then I set about making my mental prayer. I received such downpours

of grace that I was astonished. God was pleased
to sow His grace in soil the most uncultivated.
I was so changed that I seemed a different man.
The world then seemed to me an arid desert,
and I to be living on another planet.[12]

Through the grace he received, Dominic began to
wonder whether he should become a Passionist himself. The idea dimmed; he was struck down by a
serious illness and recovered some of his religious
enthusiasm. With the possibility of his having to
endure conscription for Napoleon's army he made
a conditional vow that he would join the Passionists should he be spared military service. He was
fortunate. Those who were to be conscripted were
chosen by drawing lots and Dominic picked one of
the highest numbers, 123, which exempted him from
being called up—forty thousand young men from
the Papal States were, only two thousand surviving
the battles they had to endure.

In his autobiography Dominic writes at some
length of the final years before he joined the Passionists. He describes how his religious zeal to
become a Passionist melted with his love for a
young lady of his village and of how his uncle and
the parish priest tried to persuade him to marry
her. Only with great difficulty and after many a
tussle between the competing desires of his heart
did Dominic finally succumb to the invitation of
God to enter the religious life when it finally was
possible once more to do so. At this time, he experienced mystical voices and visions, phenomena that

he had known before but which were now growing steadily stronger:

> One morning after Holy Communion I heard an interior message which was expressed in clearly defined ideas, and all I could do was just listen. I did not hear spoken words, but only ideas; and what I heard was this 'my son I want you all for Myself. You must be mine entirely. I want to be able to do as I like with you, and all you have to do, is not to resist my grace. Fear not. I am not calling you to torment you. Don't imagine that I am going to ask you to endure terrible torments, or that I want you to live as an anchorite. No, materially you will be better off than you were. All I want from you is that you do My will.[13]

Fr Dominic wrote,

> These divine messages continued for two or three months, and all I had to do in prayer was to kneel down and just listen to the voice that spoke to me. I was on such easy terms with God that He seemed, if I might put it that way, to treat me as an equal.[14]

This last statement caused one of Blessed Dominic's biographers, Alfred Wilson, to compare Dominic's understanding of his experience with a similar statement of St Theresa, 'Though He is ever my Lord, yet can I deal with Him as with an equal Friend', and with a comment of G. K. Chesterton when he said that 'Jesus is more human than humanity!'[15] During these months Dominic was given a fulsome knowledge of the consolations of faith: 'Of Himself,

God revealed to me only His mercy. I never thought about His justice or anything else; I was exclusively absorbed in contemplating His mercy.' Dominic lived in 'a sea of delights'.[16]

> Everything that I saw seemed to speak to me of God. All His creatures were messengers of the divine goodness. I continued to work in the fields, but I was always immersed in God. Sometimes I chatted with God, and sometimes, following my heart's impulse, I composed hymns to help me sing the praises of His infinite goodness.[17]

Having never received a formal education, Dominic assumed that he would become a Passionist Brother, not a priest. But soon he heard God calling him, despite this, to the priesthood. Blessed Dominic left two accounts of receiving this interior guidance, a shorter one in his autobiography and a longer version in a text entitled *Arcana Verba* which he wrote at Oscott and is dated 31 May 1844. In the first account he recalled,

> One of these days (I think it was one of the last of the year 1813) as I was saying my prayers, I heard a voice which said to me, 'I have chosen you to announce the truths of the faith to many nations'. After I had heard these words, the idea came to me that God wanted me to be a priest, and that I was to go and bring the light of the Gospel to a foreign nation. The idea pleased me.[18]

In the second record of this time he wrote,

Born as I was and brought up among poor country people, destitute of learning and the means of acquiring it, and moreover full of sins and miseries, I could never imagine that God designed me to do anything for His glory. My whole desire at the time was that God would deign to furnish His Church with good pastors, and that He would defend her against the attack of enemies who were then plotting to suppress her, especially in 1813. Towards the end of that year, one evening during the Christmas season at about 7 o'clock, I was on my knees before God in my poor little room, praying and beseeching Him to provide for the necessities of His Church, when I heard an interior voice (which only those who have heard can understand) using set words, which did not leave a shadow of a doubt as to its being from God. The voice told me that I was destined to announce the truths of the Gospel and bring back stray sheep to the way of salvation. It did not specify to me how, where, or when, or to whom—whether infidels, heretics, or bad Catholics—but left a hazy notion in my mind that the mission in store for me in the future would not be among Catholics only. I was astonished at such an announcement, and could not for the life of me imagine how it could ever be verified. However, because I felt that I could not doubt that the communication came from God, I could not doubt for an instant that it would be fulfilled.[19]

Prudently, Dominic kept all this to himself whilst wondering how such a message as he had received could come about. Ever trustful in Divine Providence, he did not concern himself with how he might be made ready for the mission that had been announced to him but rather he concentrated on such preparations as were within his immediate grasp.

One such area of groundwork was learning Latin. Dominic obtained a Latin Bible and a Latin dictionary—but no grammar book—and began, during evenings after work, to try to make sense of what he read. Undoubtedly aided by his incredible memory, though he attributed his progress to Our Lady's assistance, he soon became proficient in the language, discovering, as he went, the spiritual sense of the scriptures as well.

At this time the unparalleled sweetness of his prayer life became a more dramatic terrain.

> I began to suffer from severe and horrible temptations against faith and purity, atrocious temptations such as I had never before experienced. These temptations continued for some time; then the Lord renewed His visits and silenced them all. Until I became a religious, He continued to make alternate visitations of temptation and consolation. One day I seemed to be in hell, and the next day in Heaven. During this period, I had a suspension [ecstatic rapture] several times, during which I seemed to take leave of the senses and behold the Majesty of God under a symbol. This happened even when I was fully awake and terrified me so much that I was afraid to be alone, especially at night. Sometimes the Divinity seemed present to me, not under a definite symbol, but rather as a diffused splendour. These experiences lasted for a very brief space of time, and then

I returned to myself terrified by the sight of a majesty so great, so terrible, so immense, and yet so consoling. I began to form a more comprehensive idea of God, for up to then, I had only considered Him as mercy. Until I became a religious, I never spoke of these experiences to anyone, partly because of my reluctance to do so, and partly because they would neither have understood nor believed.[20]

✢ 3 ✢

Postulancy

F INALLY THE DAY CAME WHEN, with Napoleon
greatly weakened by his disastrous 1812
campaign against Russia, the community life
of religious orders could be restored and the Passionists returned from Merlano to their house, or
Retreat as their community houses are called, of
Sant' Angelo in Vetralla. Immediately Dominic followed them seeking admittance as a lay-postulant,
the preparatory phase for those seeking to live their
lives as non-ordained Passionist Brothers. At first,
he was rebutted as the novitiate had not yet been
formally reopened, but about a month later he was
invited to return. One of the Passionist Fathers recommended that Dominic should be admitted as a
cleric to prepare for ordination but the Provincial
was adamant that as Dominic had been accepted as
a lay brother, this was the state of life for which he
should prepare. This was the tradition of the Passionists and just in case there was any doubt about
this the Provincial also decreed that Dominic was
forbidden to study. Dominic never doubted that he
was to be called to be a priest yet as the question

was firmly in the hands of others, he did not worry himself as to how it might happen.

About this time Dominic had an experience that was to profoundly shape not only his future but, ultimately, the spiritual lives of many:

> About the end of September, or beginning of October, 1814, on a certain day, as the religious were taking their meal, I went for a few minutes into the church to pray before the altar of the Blessed Virgin, and whilst I was on my knees, the thought occurred to me—how was the prophecy of last year to be fulfilled? Was I to go as a lay-brother to preach, and to whom I was to go? China and America came to my mind. Whilst I was thus racking my brain, I understood (not by an internal locution as before, but by another mode of interior communication which I cannot explain) that I was not to remain a Brother, but was to study; and that, after six years, I should begin my apostolic ministry; and that I was not to labour either in China or America, but in the north-west of Europe, and especially in England. The time was not explained to me, and neither was the manner in which I was to be sent there. I was so convinced of this being a divine communication, that I would sooner have doubted my own existence than its truth. Soon I was sent to Paliano, to be received as a lay-novice, and yet I felt that I would, not withstanding, become a cleric and a priest.[21]

The particular altar where Dominic knelt was most significant as it was most probably at that very altar that St Paul of the Cross had seen a vision of his Passionist priests working in England. Today a marble plaque over the altar records Blessed Dominic's profound experience in the place. St Paul's vision was the culmination of a lifetime that had been marked by his constant prayers of intercession for England. Indeed, the saint had begged many who heard him preach to pray for England, instructing the houses of the Passionists to do the same. All this began when, on the Feast of St Stephen in 1720 St Paul reflected upon the sadness of England being deprived of the presence of the Eucharist. The providential nature of Blessed Dominic's experience being in perfect continuity with that of St Paul of the Cross was to make a profound impression some decades later on St John Henry Newman as he made his final approach to being received into the Catholic Church.

✦ 4 ✦

Novitiate

WITH HIS POSTULANCY OF THREE MONTHS complete, Dominic was sent with three others to begin his novitiate at the retreat of Our Lady at Paliano, a small town 60 miles south of Rome. The young men broke their journey from Vetralla by staying overnight at the Passionist retreat of Ss John and Paul in Rome. This basilica has two significant English connections: the portico of the basilica was constructed under the direction of Pope Adrian IV, the only English pope, and, before the Passionists, the church and its monastery were briefly a house of the English Dominicans thanks to the efforts of Cardinal Philip Howard (1629–94). Here at Ss John and Paul, Dominic and his companions met Bishop John Milner (1772–1826), Vicar Apostolic of the Midland District. Milner was almost certainly the first Englishman whom Dominic had ever met, and that this opportunity came within weeks of his inner locution regarding working in England was a fact not lost on him. The postulants sought the bishop's blessing before continuing on their way.

Dominic was greatly blessed in finding at Paliano a particularly holy and wise novice master, Fr Bernard of Our Lady of Sorrows (1777–1857). Very quickly Fr Bernard discerned that Dominic should be destined for priestly ordination. Fr Bernard tested Dominic's Latin on a number of occasions, two being particularly notable. The first of these occurred during evening recreation when Fr Bernard decided to question the novices about the passage from the Scriptures which had been read in Latin during supper. Whilst none of the other novices had understood the text Dominic was able to recall it, translate it and give a reflection upon it as well. Accepting humiliations were, at the time, a formal test of religious vocations so immediately Fr Bernard tested Dominic in this way as well; 'I said that he was an impudent fellow to attempt to explain Sacred Scripture in the presence of his betters. He knelt down, took the humiliation in good part and never said a word.'[22] Fr Bernard was doubly impressed.

On a later occasion Fr Bernard explicitly asked Dominic whether he would like to be a cleric. Dominic responded that he only sought the will of God and of his superiors. Fr Bernard then gave him a psalm and two passages, one from Scripture and the other from the life of St Charles Borromeo, to translate from Latin into Italian. Dominic simply recorded that 'I did this and took back my papers to him'.[23] Fr Bernard, however, later recalled that it took Dominic only a quarter of an hour to make an excellent translation, indeed, he wrote, 'he made a

better translation than I could have made myself'.[24]
With the approval of the General of the Passionists
(the head of the order) a vote of all the priests of the
community at Paliano was held and, unanimously,
the Fathers voted for Dominic to be accepted as a
cleric preparing for Holy Orders.

Dominic received the Passionist habit on 14
November 1814, being given the name of Dominic
of the Mother of God. During his novitiate Dominic
not only remembered to pray for England himself
but was keen to encourage his confreres to do so too.
Many years later Fr Bernard left a written record of
his impressions of Dominic during his novitiate:

> He was the most diligent, exact and fervent of
> all the novices in the observance of the Rule.
> Most fervent of all, too, in prayer, mortification,
> recollection and in learning the practice of
> virtue. I never had to tell him anything twice.
> He was also, I should add, cheerful, frank, light-
> hearted and yet solid. As far as I could judge,
> he preserved his baptismal innocence, and I
> am persuaded that he preserved it till death,
> and adorned it, moreover, with ever-increasing
> virtue, especially with the virtue of humility,
> which caused him to regard himself as the
> vilest man on earth and unworthy of human
> society. To humility, he united utter contempt
> for himself and for anything that smacked of
> worldliness or sensuality. He burned with zeal
> for the glory of God and the salvation of souls,
> especially for those outside the Church, and
> for them, he studied, thought, wrote, worked
> and prayed. At table he was so recollected as to
> hardly notice what he was eating; a fact which

I was able to confirm years later when I lived in his community. This is all I can say about Fr Dominic of the Mother of God, and I can say it without any fear of having exaggerated.

Fr Bernard lived to a great age, surviving Dominic by many years. In his latter years a fellow religious asked him about Dominic Barberi and with eyes alight, and tears rolling down his cheeks, he replied, 'I can't find words good enough to describe him'.[25]

✢ 5 ✢

Further Studies

H AVING COMPLETED HIS NOVITIATE, Dominic
was sent to the Retreat of the Presentation
on Monte Argentaro, the first monastery
founded by St Paul of the Cross. In the beauty of
this place, set on the Mediterranean coast, he was to
spend a year under the direction of Fr John Peter, a
priest of whom Passionist records relate 'combined
sublime knowledge with singular piety'.[26] At Monte
Argentaro Dominic continued his studies before
being sent to the mother-house of Ss John and Paul
at Rome.

In Rome Dominic's director and principal professor was a priest that he already knew well, Fr
Anthony of St James, a Passionist who was to lead
his order and ultimately be considered as its second
founder. Dominic studied hard and made astonishing progress very quickly. His first biographer and
one-time companion, Fr Filippo of the Annunciation,
recalled that

> He was gifted with a keen penetrating mind, and
> clarity of ideas was second nature to him. He
> had, moreover, an exceptional memory which

was both quick and retentive. He remembered what he had heard or read twenty or thirty years before as accurately as if he had just heard or read it, and even quoted statements made then verbatim. To these rare gifts he united a keen thirst for knowledge and exceptional powers of concentration. As a result, he made astonishing progress in study; however, in his humility and cult of self-contempt, he always strove to take the last place, and was more scared of appearing learned than others are of appearing ignorant. Because of this ingenious humility, his companions never suspected his singular brilliance, and when it first began to sparkle during the early years of his ministry, they were astounded.[27]

Among his confreres there was, as Dominic's learning came to the fore, some discussion about the source of his knowledge and wisdom. Some attributed it to supernaturally infused knowledge, others noted his superb memory and perseverance in attaining the required ends. Dominic himself seems to have acknowledged both, believing that anything good he did was because of God's grace and that he had a great capacity and desire to learn, perhaps, he thought, too great a desire: 'The root of my numerous imperfections,' he noted, 'is immoderate thirst for knowledge; to check this, I will strive to know nothing but Jesus.'[28] Having so resolved, we can be sure that Dominic so did, as there appears to be little discrepancy between what he wrote privately as he assessed and discerned the motions of his heart and what he then went on to do. He recorded many such resolutions in his diary:

> This year in imitation of St Felix, the Capuchin,
> I will regard myself as the Passionist's donkey,
> unworthy to live with others, and I will take
> upon myself the most laborious duties.
>
> I will reverence all as my betters, or rather
> as Jesus himself ... I will obey and serve them,
> whenever I can do so legitimately.
>
> I will learn something from each of them,
> from Fr Ambrose, resignation to God's holy
> will; from Fr John Matthew, perseverance in
> study.

A long list of the virtues that Fr Dominic saw in his
confreres follows, virtues which Fr Dominic was
determined to emulate himself. 'Every day, among
other graces, I will ask this one—to suffer, to be
humiliated and made no account of, for the love of
Jesus.'[29]

As his first biographer records,

> His quondam fellow-student attests that
> in Confrater Dominic, self-hatred, love of
> mortification and self-contempt had to be
> restrained to prevent excess. Self-hatred made
> him invariably seek the last place. He tried to
> reserve to himself all the domestic offices that
> are usually portioned out among the students.
> When heavy and disagreeable duties were
> assigned to him in preference to someone
> else, he was overjoyed. On Saturday evenings
> when it is the custom for the students to do the
> household chores, he hurried to finish his own
> work, and then, without waiting to be asked,
> went to give a hand to anyone who was behind
> with his work or had too much to do.

If the superior gave an order to the students as a body, Dominic always took it as meant for him, and immediately executed it. One could sum up everything by saying that he effectively considered himself the servant of all, and acted as such on every occasion.[30]

Dominic drew up a rigorous rule of life for himself that was full to bursting with devotions from dawn to dusk. He also recorded his failures:

I have fallen off in many things. At table, I have occasionally taken more than was strictly necessary. During recreation, I have sometimes sought out those who are congenial to me, and avoided those who irritate me. Now and then, I have hurried when celebrating Mass. When asked to do an act of charity, on occasion I have shown reluctance. During the community recreation, I have sometimes been taciturn, and made no attempt to cheer up the downhearted. My thoughts have strayed to my writings during prayer and the Divine Office. Reform in all these things or they will ruin me. Mary most holy, help me. I have fallen off in obedience to my companions, and for that reason Our Lord has sometimes withheld His visits.[31]

And so he resolved:

In future, provided I can do so without sin, I will always obey my companions, no matter how disagreeable their requests may be, nor how much they upset my plans, even plans for study. Whenever an opportunity to help someone turns up, I will cheerfully sacrifice study, and show no sign of reluctance. If I am called to the confessional, I will go at once, and even leave a sentence unfinished.[32]

All this might bring one to assume that Dominic was a somewhat humourless young cleric whereas he seems to have been both an assiduous young Passionist and a very jolly one too. His diary records him accusing himself of undue levity, a tendency to tease others and an ability to chatter too much. It also records his great devotion to the saints whose particular virtues he sought to emulate:

> St John the Evangelist, my first patron since childhood will obtain for me great charity for my neighbour and perfect purity; St Mary Magdalene will obtain for me sorrow for sin and compassion for Jesus crucified;
>
> St Joseph and St Theresa, the spirit of prayer;
>
> St Francis Xavier and St Vincent de Paul, zeal for the glory of God;
>
> St Francis of Assisi, love of poverty, simplicity and devotion to the Passion;
>
> St Aloysius, the spirit of penance;
>
> St Paul the Apostle, love of Jesus, zeal for the conversion of sinners and the grace to be all things to all men;
>
> St Gregory the Great, dedication to the conversion of England;
>
> St David, devotion to reciting the Divine Office and sorrow for sin;
>
> My Angel Guardian, recollection and alertness to God's presence;
>
> St Dominic, devotion to Mary and her Rosary;
>
> St Francis de Sales, the spirit of meekness.[33]

The years of preparation for priesthood over, Dominic was ordained on 1 March 1818 in the private chapel of Archbishop Candido Maria Frattini (1767–1821), then vice-gerent of Rome.

✛ 6 ✛

Light and Darkness

S HORTLY AFTER ORDINATION Dominic recorded
his deepest feelings in pages entitled *A Dialogue between a Young Priest and the Blessed Virgin Mary*. 'On the day of my ordination', he wrote,
'the torrent of my delight was so overwhelming that
I was afraid of being suffocated.' As for the day of
his first Mass,

> Virgin most holy, you understand. There is
> no need to tell you. As I handled the Sacred
> Host, how can I describe what I experienced?
> You alone could describe it who handled that
> divine Body so worthily. But as for me, how do
> I treat it? Ah, my heavenly Mother, that is what
> horrifies me. How different would it be, if I had
> your purity, your sanctity! When I am about to
> celebrate, how I long to have your heart as a
> fitting resting place for my Jesus; your hands
> with which to touch Him; and your voice to
> summon Him to the holy altar. But I have neither
> your hands, nor your heart. Far from it, I am a
> mass of iniquity, and I tremble at the thought.
> And yet, Jesus my Lord and my God, is so kind!
> He allows me to deal with Him as He did the
> cruel executioners who nailed Him to the cross.

I say to Him: 'My Jesus, behold in me Judas, Your executioner, Your crucifier.' And yet He is not offended by all this. He takes pleasure, it almost seems, in being treated like this by me a miserable wretch. Instead of reproving me for my temerity in approaching Him, He even appears to invite me, and is wistful to enter my unworthy heart.[34]

Our Lady encourages Dominic to have confidence in his ministry:

Imagine that you are receiving Him, as I received Him in my womb when He was incarnate, or as I welcomed Him to my arms when He was born, or as I embraced Him on the road to Calvary: or again, as I received Him into my arms when they took Him down from the Cross ... Remember too, as you say Mass, that it is your duty not only to offer the Holy Sacrifice, but also to pray for all Christian people, for the Church, for the conversion of sinners, and for the salvation of all those whom God assigns to your care as children to their father.[35]

Dominic responds,

This I will do to the utmost of my power. From the moment I was ordained priest, I think so much of the salvation of others that I almost seem to have forgotten myself. How willingly would I see all saved, all saints. If I could give my blood, every drop of it, for the conversion of sinners, I would gladly do so, but what profit is there in my blood? [To which the Virgin replies,] 'If your blood is of no avail, the Blood of Jesus, which you receive, is mighty to save. Offer it, then my son, for the conversion of poor sinners and of heretics; remember that they too are my children, redeemed by the Precious Blood of my divine Son.' [Dominic:] 'Yes, from this day forward, my one thought, my loving task, shall be to carry out your commands.'[36]

Written on loose sheets of paper and only discovered after Dominic's death, *A Dialogue between a Young Priest and the Blessed Virgin Mary* reads as if it records a real event. Certainly it is in the tradition of the Passionists, and is frequently mentioned in Blessed Dominic's process for beatification, that this dialogue took place in the domestic chapel of the retreat at Ss John and Paul and that the painting of the Madonna over the altar there indeed did speak to Fr Dominic.

The two years immediately after Dominic's ordination were flooded with happiness and blessings: he was rapturously happy.

This morning I experienced intense feelings of love of Jesus and realized how absolutely one ought to be entirely His. I burned with desire to make all love Him, no matter what trials the attempt to do so might cost me, since I am always safe when hidden in Him. I will strive never to be parted from Him, and whenever His glory is at stake, even if I have to sacrifice my life a thousand times over, I will not flinch.[37]

Whenever an opportunity of practising virtue presents itself, I will imagine that I see Jesus before me, requesting me to do this for love of Him; and then I shall never dare to say 'no' to Him to His face.[38]

My Jesus! Would that I could annihilate myself, if by so doing, I could contribute even a little to

Your glory; Would that my voice could make itself heard to the ends of the earth crying to all, 'Love Jesus Christ, Love Jesus Christ'.[39]

Having received so much of the sweetness of the knowledge and feeling of God's presence in his life, Dominic offered to exchange all this for the conversion of souls declaring 'My God, keep your graces. You know that this is not what I want. Give me instead the conversion of souls.'[40]

His prayer was heard. In June 1820 Dominic accepted from God the very opposite of the experiences of His closeness that he had known since his ordination. In the midst of his prayer Dominic was invited by the Lord to live the remainder of his life by the light of faith alone: his was to know spiritual aridity and darkness, no more comforting experiences of the presence of God for him. This was a degree of testing such as few are asked to bear: St John of the Cross knew the Dark Night of the soul, but that was to pass. Blessed Dominic of the Mother of God's experience was to be akin to that known also by St Teresa of Calcutta (as revealed after her death in her diary) which was ultimately being granted a share in the experience of the abandonment and desolation of Christ in His Passion and Death. 'Do you mean, my God that I shall have to endure forever the awful agony that prostrates my heart now?', asked Dominic: the silence of God confirmed this. 'Lord, if it be possible, let this chalice pass from me; yet not my will but Thine be done.' responded Dominic. For the rest of his life just the remembrance of this decisive moment caused him immense anguish.[41] Sixteen years later Dominic described his mystical experience:

> My God, what agony I experienced then. My soul seemed to be torn from my body, no it was more than that, I think that if my soul had been torn from my body, I should not have experienced such pain. It was rather as if the soul was torn from the soul; even that does not describe it, it was more, more ... I experienced a pain so lively, so penetrating, so fierce, such as I have never experienced before. I believe that only the sorrow of the damned of hell can exceed that pain ... I seemed about to swoon ... I know not how I managed to live through it.[42]

As Alfred Wilson rightly observes, 'There can be no doubt that that momentous sacrifice was a cardinal event of his life ... and the apotheosis of his mysterious calls at Merlano and Saint Angelo'. Wilson continues, 'In imitation of his Divine Master, he [Dominic] was to contribute to the world's redemption, not primarily by preaching, but by suffering and mystical death'. Indeed, 'His considerable, but by no means commensurate, ministerial success was not the principal purpose nor the major fruit of his supernatural vocation. Unless that is understood, his singular vocation might be dismissed as much ado about very little.'[43]

In his commentary on the Song of Songs, *Il Gemito della Colomba* (The Moaning of the Dove), Fr Dominic describes aspects of the soul in the torments of spiritual abandonment:

You inflicted this wound on my heart, and You alone can heal it. Since that is the case, why did you go away?...Since You know my impotence, either You should not have revealed Yourself as You did, or You should have stayed with me, or at least have freed me from life and taken me with You.[44]

What do I seek on earth and in heaven? You alone are my good, my treasure, my all. You alone can satisfy my desires, You alone I desire. Ah! If only my sighs could hasten the steps of death.[45]

It cannot, it cannot, a tiny heart cannot love a God so great and immense. And for me this is a state of continual martyrdom; such a martyrdom that if it lasts I can't see myself living long. And what shall I do, my God, to be able to bear this pain? I would wish to cry out, I would wish to invite all men.[46]

As a Passionist himself Alfred Wilson comments, 'Abandoned in this terrifying darkness, he was able to penetrate more deeply into the soul-splitting agony of Gethsemane, and the awful desolation and dereliction of Calvary'. This really constituted Fr Dominic in the closest alignment to the Eternal Priesthood of Jesus Christ, Priest and Victim: 'Like St Paul of the Cross, he was a practitioner and apostle of mystical death, a Passionist in a terrifying sense', wrote Wilson.[47] In his diary, on 12 June 1820, Fr Dominic recorded,

Our Lord has made it clear to me that I am to serve Him *without any sweetness*; and in the presence of Mary most holy, of my holy advocates and of my Guardian Angel, I have promised that in future I will consider Him alone and strive to love Him without any thought of self, so that my heart may always be united to Him, and that I may love Him no matter how desolate I may be, seeing that He is always equally lovable. I desire to think of nothing but Him. Once more I renounce the joy of His blessed presence and every consolation both spiritual and sensible, except that of seeing His Name known and venerated by all, which I will pray for unceasingly. No matter how great my aridity may be, I will never cease to pray for the salvation of my brethren, and I protest that I will never cease praying for this intention until I see God's name known and honoured through the world, and especially until I see England reunited to the Church. When I do not know what else to do, I will offer the merits of Jesus Christ to the Heavenly Father for this intention.[48]

Three months later, having begun to grow accustomed to his new spiritual state, Fr Dominic once more confided in his diary:

In this month of October I have experienced a great longing for the conversion of unbelievers, especially of England, and I have offered myself to God to be annihilated, if annihilation could serve this purpose. I must make sure that this desire is never extinguished, for I am certain that, if I persevere, God will be moved to pity. I intend now, in the presence of God, to ratify all my former promises. Lord, if you wish me to go mad, or to be unfrocked or hung, or ostracized from human society; if You wish to annul me; if You wish to condemn me to Purgatory until the day of Judgement, if You wish to deprive me of Your sensible help, if You wish that I should never enjoy any satisfaction in prayer, or that I should be tormented by scruples; if You wish to condemn me to suffer all the pains that the English would have to suffer if they were damned I am content, provided only that they all return to You. My God, I protest that I will never allow my heart any consolation until I witness their conversion. If You desire to give me a proof of Your love, open the way to their conversion, in whatever way pleases You. I do not ask this through any merits of my own, but through the merits of the Precious Blood shed by Your Divine Son, through the merits of Mary Most Holy, and through the intercession of all the saints in Heaven. My dear Mother, now it is up to you to obtain this for me. I want it, and all I want is the glory of Your Divine Son and the salvation of my brethren, 'Fratres meos quaero'. You are my mother so give me this proof of it; I can enjoy nothing until you do. Don't let this be the first time that I have had refusal from you. The glory will be yours and your Divine Son's for all eternity, Amen.[49]

Again, Alfred Wilson clearly saw that 'That love-crazy prayer is tantamount to an expression of readiness to sacrifice anything, or put up with anything, for the sake of his beloved English. Obviously, he was enumerating the worst trials that he could think of, and offering to endure any or all of them for England's sake. He meant every word of it.'[50]

What was left for Fr Dominic's feelings during prayer? Very little. 'If, occasionally, I find a little inspiration apart from my meditation on the Passion', he wrote to a friend, 'I consider myself extremely fortunate.'[51] And when he found he felt that he could not pray, he prayed all the same, saying the words of the Our Father meditatively, often repeating the words 'hallowed be Thy Name' or just saying again and again 'Ita, Pater',—'So be it, Father'. He sought solace in the favours of the past, but found the feeling of their loss even more heart-breaking:

> Gone are the happy times when I found Thee so easily. I found Thee in the manger of Bethlehem; I found Thee in Gethsemane; I found Thee on Calvary; I found and tasted Thee in the Blessed Sacrament. I gazed on Thy face, and listened to Thy supremely melodious voice. In Thy divine presence my heart melted like soft wax to become flowing oil.[52]

And so it continued until the end of his life. In his final years Fr Dominic, whilst offering guidance to an English Benedictine nun, called upon his own experience of abandonment in order to encourage the lady. She asked him if he ever expected to see God before he died. 'I don't know,' Fr Dominic replied, smiling cheerfully, according to the nun, 'anyway I am not a baby in need of sweets.'[53]

Throughout all this, Fr Dominic remained very close to the Blessed Virgin Mary through his devotions including, unfailingly, his daily recitation of the rosary. His diary very frequently invokes her maternal assistance to pursue resolutions in words such as 'Dear Mother, help me to put this into practise. Mary

most holy, help me to do it . . . Mama mine, help me.'
Resolutions seeking Our Lady's help flowed from Fr
Dominic's pen:

> Never allow a single day to pass without
> offering some flowers to Our Lady by acts of
> mortification.[54]
>
> Surrender your heart and whole person to Jesus
> and Mary, and beg them to do as they like with
> you. As a faithful lover, seek their approval of
> all your actions by avoiding whatever could
> displease them, and by doing everything
> possible to please them.[55]
>
> Every morning at Mass, present the Holy Sacrifice
> to the Heavenly Father in thanksgiving for the
> graces given to Mary. After Holy Communion
> welcome Our Lord as Mary did at the moment
> of the Incarnation. Every Saturday, make a
> special remembrance of Our Lady's Sorrows
> and try to really enter into them.
>
> Grant this Lord (i.e. the conversion of
> England), for the love you bear to Mary
> most Holy. From eternity you have crowned
> her with glory. Let not this occasion pass of
> enriching her diadem with these new gems—
> the souls for whom Christ died. If you grant
> the return of England to the Catholic Faith,
> churches will spring up there in her honour,
> and converts will sing her praises and recite
> her Rosary.
>
> My Lord and my God! open the doors of Your
> mercy to that island. Here in the presence of
> the Blessed Virgin, I promise that if you grant
> me a part in a work so glorious, I will always
> work and toil that Mary be known, loved and
> invoked, by all.[56]

Fr Dominic's total confidence in the maternal protection of Our Lady, seen both from a natural and supernatural point of view, inspired a childlike trust in her affection and protection:

> Cultivate heartfelt affection for the most Holy Virgin and let out your affections on her. Don't stand on ceremony, but be a real baby; hug her, embrace her feet, offer your heart to her and above all ask for perseverance. But don't show your love only in words; show it by deeds, and present flowers of virtue to her, eg. mortification of curiosity for love of her. Small things, granted; but they will not be small if they give pleasure to Mary and weave a crown of merit for heaven.[57]

> With a mother, and such a mother, boldness is love's fondling; with such a mother every true son is daring. You put up with me in my bad days; you will put up with me now, even when I am a nuisance.[58]

Given that Fr Dominic always said that impurity was always one of his besetting temptations, it is surprising that there are but three reference to the subject in the diary where he confided his innermost thoughts and prayers:

> In every temptation, especially in those against purity, do not panic or make frantic efforts to resist, particularly if you are trying to get to sleep. Keep calm, say a prayer of love, kiss and hug the crucifix, and then settle down again to sleep.[59]

> When I experience movements of concupiscence, I will humble myself and marvel that God should have suffered so much for one so vile.

I will draw from the temptation an argument for the amazing love of God, and say with St Paul: 'gladly will I glory in my infirmities'.[60]

When I am in the houses of seculars, I will not look at the pictures, lest I see immodest ones which may afterwards give me cause to weep.[61]

Fr Dominic's devotion to the Mother of God was given expression in prayer that crystalizes his estimation of himself, and his appreciation of her:

O greatest, most noble, most amiable, most loving, most pure, most holy of pure creatures, behold at your feet the most miserable of beings, the most unworthy of your sons, yes the most unworthy, but at the same time the son of your love, of your tenderness and of your mercy. Relying on your maternal goodness, I come to you most trustfully ... My mother, my tender Mother, let us work together for the salvation of souls and the glory of God, for love of Jesus, your Divine Son.[62]

7

Professor

I N MAY 1821, at the age of 28, Fr Dominic was appointed professor of philosophy and direc-tor of students at Sant' Angelo. The General, Fr Paolo Luigi, told him that he was second choice—his first preference was too unwell to take up the post— but this did not diminish Fr Dominic's happiness in taking up his allotted task in the house where he had first entered the Passionist order. Unsurprisingly, he flung himself into his new work, being compared, by his first biographer, to a torrent in full flood.[63]

Armed with his prodigious memory, Fr Dominic spent hours reading, and to a large extent memo-rizing, vast tracts of philosophy, particularly paying attention to the writings of St Thomas Aquinas. 'If you want to be great', he wrote in his book of apho-risms, 'don't read small books.'[64] Thus prepared, Fr Dominic reflected upon what he read and delivered the results of his labours with lively and engaging enthusiasm. This enthusiasm could get the better of him and he would lose track of the time. To remedy this fault, he charged the future Provincial in Eng-land, Eugene Martorelli, to watch the clock and cut him short by declaring 'Brother Dominic you would do well to be silent'. Thus admonished, Dominic would fall silent, no further syllable of the lecture being given.[65]

Fr Dominic was immensely popular as a teacher, undoubtedly the result of his manner both in front of the students and among them as fellow Passionists, as a resolution that he wrote in his diary indicates:

> In the company of the students I will take good care to be always cheerful and jovial in manner and never put on a stern and serious front, but *be among them as one of them*. I will never correct a student at recreation without necessity, but strive to keep them peaceful and content.[66]

A former student is recorded as being asked whether or not he and his companions had been fond of Fr Dominic. 'Fond of him!' he cried, 'we adored him.'[67] Still, Fr Dominic was careful, resolving at the start of the 1823 academic year to always 'use mild and healing words, nor raise my voice, nor mortify unduly' when a student had to be corrected. Employing a familiar penance of the time he resolved 'If ever I do give way to anger and raise my voice when correcting, I will penance myself by licking the ground fifteen times', ensuring in future that before attempting any form of correction he would seek the assistance of Our Lady (with three Hail Marys) and St Francis de Sales (saying a further Our Father and Hail Mary).[68] 'Several times', he wrote,

> I have been at fault in my interviews with the students by letting myself get ruffled. I must

watch this, or I shall shut them up and prevent them from opening their hearts freely. A mother is not peevish when she becomes aware of her children's weaknesses. My God, give me a mother's heart, especially for those who depend on me.[69]

Remembered as kind and encouraging, Fr Dominic also knew when a firmer hand was needed. 'Generally he pleaded rather than corrected', recalled one former student; 'On rare occasions, however, especially of disobedience or pig-headedness, he could be very forthright and make one sit up and remember what was said for a very long time.'[70]

For himself, Fr Dominic knew that he had to be watchful that his love of study did not eclipse his spiritual life. 'I must not allow myself to become obsessed by the itch to write' he wrote, accusing himself of writing too much. 'Always prefer exercises of piety to study', he concludes, 'because they are the means to the principal end.'[71] But clearly he valued academic work and was in no doubt as to its necessity for those preparing for priesthood. Such knowledge, he wrote 'is not infused, nor can one expect it to be infused, there is no other way of acquiring it than by sweat, assiduous vigils and tireless study'.[72]

During his scholastic course the student learns how to study, but real study is done afterwards during the rest of his life. 'But how can one find time to study then? There are always a thousand and one things to be done, and they must be done diligently.' Yet I assure you that if you make up your mind, you can always find time for study, and even time for study of Scripture and the Fathers. If you are lovers of silence and the cell; if you are averse to wasting time in trifles, as for example, in devouring newspapers, poems, profane antiquities and such like time-wasters, you will find the time needed; believe one who speaks from experience. Certainly I have had no more spare time than others, nor have I a 34 hour day, and yet I have managed to do something, and do it without ever failing to execute the orders of my superiors. Time can be found when goodwill is not lacking.[73]

Whilst seeing that prayer must hold first place in the young Passionists' hearts, Fr Dominic rejected the idea that

study chills devotion and damps the spirit ... In this, St Thomas is my guide both in his learning and, even more, in his example. How great was his elevation of mind, how intense his application to the most sublime studies, and how great his devotion, his fervour, his tenderness towards God! All the same, this holy doctor himself points out that although study does not, *per se*, diminish devotion and fervour, it often does so, *per accidens*, not through any fault of study, but through the fault of students.[74]

Study of the Scriptures was paramount for Fr Dominic having himself resolved to give at least half an hour every day to reading the Bible saying, 'I will make it my food and my refuge in every temptation'.[75] In close second place in his affections was spiritual reading that was either written by the saints or accounts of their lives.[76] His preferred authors were St Paul of the Cross, St John of the Cross, St Francis de Sales and St Mary Magdalene de Pazzi.

Yet, in the midst of teaching, reading, writing and, of course praying, Fr Dominic found time to continue his Latin studies and teach himself Greek, French and basic English. He also encouraged his students to engage with and evangelize the wood-cutters and charcoal burners that they would meet on their walks through the woods. This was, for the time, an enterprising approach as usually a very segregated existence was demanded of clerical students. The young men would strike up conversations with those that they met, gathering small groups for informal instruction which was concluded by Fr Dominic gathering together all the little groups and preaching to them himself using the stump of a tree as a pulpit.[77] He also sent students to the local hospital to visit the sick.[78]

As well as teaching philosophy, Fr Dominic preached regularly in the church at Sant' Angelo. His preaching was simple and sincere, practical and homely, salted with gentle humour. Likewise, in the confessional he was known for his unfailing kindness and wisdom—he would spend hours on end hearing confessions, drawing many nearby clergy to his confessional. Out of the abundance of his heart his words were capable of entering in and resonating in the souls of both his brother priests and of men and women who had received no formal education. 'Father, what was the name of the priest who preached on the last feast-day?', Fr Dominic was once asked, 'How well he preached! One could follow every single word.' The preacher was Fr Dominic.[79] On another occasion he was asked, 'Who preached last Sunday? . . . whoever he was he was a poor hand at it.' 'What makes you think so?' asked Fr Dominic. 'Well, just imagine, even I could follow every word he said. He must be a very poor scholar if he could talk for an hour without using a single word not too big for a pate like mine.' Again, the preacher was Fr Dominic.[80]

Despite all this activity, Fr Dominic was also first to offer help when and where it was needed be it acting as porter looking after the pigs or the horses, helping in the kitchen or chopping the wood. He hardly ever complained if he felt put upon by others but, in his diary, he recorded one occasion when, in front of the students, he complained to the Rector of the retreat that he really should not have to act as the community's porter every day. He was almost certainly right in what he said and the tone of voice in which he would have said it but yet, having examined his conscience, he found that he had not lived up to the perfection to which every Christian is called:

> God has made me realise the harm that I have done, and that this is a punishment for my pride in boasting to the students that I have never complained about duties imposed on me by my superiors. With God's help, I now propose never again to say anything that could redound to my credit, and never to complain to superiors, especially when others are present. If

ever a mitigation of an order seems called for,
I will refer the matter to the superior when no
one else is present.[81]

8

Writing

I N THE MIDST OF EVERYTHING SO FAR OUTLINED Fr Dominic was writing at immense speed many, many books. On returning from a walk he would go straight to his desk to jot down any ideas that had come to his mind during his exercise. Amongst the manuscripts that he wrote during his five years at Sant' Angelo are

- a volume of sermons on the Christian's life (for country-folk);
- a volume of sermons on the Sunday Gospels;
- a volume of sermons on the feasts of the liturgical year;
- five courses of sermons for religious;
- two volumes of Mission sermons and one of outlines;
- two courses of catechetical instructions on Confessions and the Commandments;
- separate volumes of sermons for the laity, clergy and religious respectively;
- the *Via Passionis*, a devotional work on the Passion;
- the *Anima Guidata*, a book of meditations on the life and Passion of the Lord;

- *Il Celeste Pedagogo*, instructions for a young religious;
- the *Marialogia*;
- and volumes of sermons on the Passion of Christ and the Sorrows of Our Lady.

This is not an exhaustive list. In the Passionist archives in Rome there are 100 volumes of manuscripts containing 180 works, yet it is thought that a third of Blessed Dominic's writings are missing.

It was during his time at Sant' Angelo that Fr Dominic read the Confessions of St Augustine and the spiritual autobiography of St Theresa of Avila. Having read these works he wondered whether he should also commit to paper his own life story. Realising that this might merely be an expression of his ego he submitted the idea to his confessor, Fr Luigi of St Anne. Fr Luigi gave a clear instruction that Fr Dominic was to write his autobiography and start doing so without delay. This Dominic took literally and, as he continued giving his first community retreat in 1822, he began in the hope that 'the recording and re-consideration of God's immense favours to me will inspire me to dedicate myself wholeheartedly to His Divine Majesty and to be converted in earnest'.[82] He entitled his work *Outline of the Divine Mercy in the Conversion of a Sinner*.

When Fr Dominic had completed his autobiography he handed it, in a sealed envelope, to Fr Luigi with the request that it not be opened until after his death. The manuscript lay unread in Fr Luigi's possession but in 1826 he feared that he might be dying so passed the sealed envelope to a confrere. Curiosity got the better of the confrere, Fr John Matthew, who opened the envelope, glancing at the manuscript. For some unknown reason — perhaps guilt? — he then handed the autobiography back to an astonished and hurt Fr Dominic who gently complained to Fr Luigi, who had not died as he had feared. Fr Dominic then hid the manuscript so well that it was thought that he had destroyed it, the work only being found over a hundred years later.

Before this debacle, during the Spiritual Exercises of 1823, Fr Dominic's confessor once again commanded that a further volume of autobiography be written. In complying with this instruction Fr Dominic sought to conceal the autobiographical nature of the work within a commentary on the first four chapters of the Song of Songs, that canticle being one of his most loved books in the Bible and one that had inspired him from his teenage years onwards. As ever the British Isles are part of his thoughts and prayers: 'The Islands are waiting, yes, they are waiting to share these delightful fruits', he mused.

Assessing all of Fr Dominic's extant writings during the process that led to his beatification, the official reader of the Congregation of Rites declared that

> It is astonishing that a man so burdened with so many responsibilities could have written so much. Without any doubt, he was an outstanding theologian ... In this mass of volumes, one can easily recognize the amazing charity of the

servant of God, who wrote almost everything by request, not for his own use, but for the use of others. In all the works that I have read and examined, the Servant of God proves himself to have been a man of intense piety, great zeal for souls and the glory of God, and a religious of exceptional perfection.[83]

The same reader, however, 'repeatedly, and rightly, objected to the severity of some of Dominic's pronouncements' as found in his earlier writings. This Fr Dominic acknowledged himself as he would delete such severe lines in his works should a manuscript ever be returned to him in later life. His true, matured spirit as a pastor can be found in the *Apparato all'Apostolico Ministro* of 1837 which includes such advice as 'Do not say, at the start of a mission, that those who neglect the grace of the mission will make their salvation impossible. Say rather "difficult". Quit that impossible',[84] and 'When speaking of death, don't say that conversion at such a time is impossible. O! Cut Out that blessed IMPOSSIBLE that is touted by so many preachers. Use instead a milder term and one more catholic.'[85] In the last work that Fr Dominic ever wrote he counselled young priests

> I want to mention here a mistake I once made, so that you may be able to avoid making it yourselves. In one place I spoke very strongly about the moral impossibility of a priest changing his way of life. After the lecture a priest came to me and said, 'Father, I had intended to change my life, but since I heard that this is almost impossible, I have decided not to try'.

He has announced nothing but suffering. Remembrance of the agony of the Spouse on the Cross constrains it to repeat, in the upper region of the soul, His selfsame words. In the stress of agony, it longs to embrace the Spouse, but He leaves it to wrestle with its agony alone. Once the soul used to embrace the Spouse without His pains; then, the pains were added; but now, it has to embrace only His pains, without being able to clasp and embrace the Spouse ... O! God, what a crucifixion it is! The soul has to suffer for the Beloved, though it is deprived of His presence, and even ignorant of His whereabouts, and while it feels as completely abandoned by the Heavenly Father as Christ was on the cross. O! bitter desolation which prepares the soul for that mystical death which is so desirable! But there is something worse, something to which the human tongue can never give utterance, nor the human mind conceive, unless it has experienced it. Nor even in hell can a parallel suffering be found. The damned suffer, but do not love; this soul, however, both loves and suffers, and love augments its pain. Its pains are as atrocious as the fire of its love is intense. Heaven, earth, hell, men, demons and passions league together to afflict it. The soul seems incapable of applying itself to anything good, and horribly tempted by lust, anger, despair and infidelity, is violently propelled towards evil. In this state it is easy for the soul to give way to impatience ... a miracle that it does not make an attempt on someone's life, or utter most execrable blasphemies ... The whole human race seems but a detestable rabble which the soul feels compelled to hate. Nevertheless, at its peak, it continues to repeat acts of pure love of

God, such as: 'You are in blessedness, and that
is enough for me. Do as you please with me.
My only happiness is in Your happiness.' This
is the mystical death which many talk about,
but few understand, though St Paul of the Cross
described it admirably. The soul is afflicted by
cold, darkness, hunger, thirst, immense toil,
terrifying sadness, the Agony and the Sweat of
Blood. Greatly daring, it deliberately chooses
these companions, and because it is aware that
the Will of God spurs it on to face these torments
alone, plunges into a pitch-black immensity
bearing its heart before it like a lighted torch.[88]

One of the effects of all this on Fr Dominic was that
he became even more self-critical than ever. He was
blessed with a wise spiritual director, Blessed Law-
rence of St Francis Xavier, who instilled in him the
need for patience with himself and, in so doing, he
also inculcated in him a spirit of mildness and compassion. Now he was able to note, as if a new thought
that had just struck him, 'If sometimes we tell God
about our foibles, He understands'.[89]

As well as fulfilling his teaching obligations, Fr
Dominic became a desired preacher for retreats,
receiving many invitations to preach during his
years in Rome. It seems that his was a conversa-
tional style of preaching, not at all typical at the time.
He was not gifted with a particularly pleasant tone
of voice—apparently it was weak and squeaky. He
loved to say that the preacher should be an invisible
man, the message of Christ not the oratorical gifts
of the speaker being uppermost to the hearer. 'The
most powerful orator', he wrote,

is not the one who is applauded, but the one who moves all to follow him. When a man is moved to repentance he thinks only of amending his life, and does not stop to praise anyone. If the people leave the church praising the preacher, one can be certain that he did not do his duty well. Sighs, not praise, are proof of effective oratory.[90]

Further remarks underscore his point: 'Flowers are good, but of no use to the starving'; 'He who speaks to the inhabitants of the stars has no effect on the inhabitants of this earth'.

The true style of oratory, and the most difficult to achieve, is that which seems simple and easy, and leaves the listener with the impression that he could have done just as well himself. The efficacy of preaching lies in plain, natural instruction about the duties of everyman.[91]

It is a rare gift to be able to touch the hearts of hearers when they are, as they can be, very diverse in terms of cultural background. To be able to do this is undoubtedly a great blessing from God. After attending a retreat that Fr Dominic gave to a group that consisted of sixteen different trades, a judge and a cardinal, the cardinal afterwards noted, 'For the life of me, I cannot understand how Fr Dominic managed to treat each subject so perfectly, and yet adapt it to that varied congregation. Certainly, I could not have done it.'[92] Fr Dominic left an account of how he went about preparing a sermon:

Whenever I begin to prepare a sermon, I will first turn to God and Mary most holy to beg for the lights necessary to enable me to lead souls to salvation by means of the word of God. I must not let myself be carried away by the desire to write learnedly and display erudition. If brilliant sayings flash into my mind, I will first ask myself if, at the hour of death, I shall be glad to have said them; and then omit them. As regards historical and profane authors, I will refrain from quoting them at all; and as to quotations, I must see to it that they are not numerous, but few and pithy, and generally from Sacred Scripture, and only from the Fathers of the Church. Fifteen at the most will suffice for one sermon, more than that would smack of ostentation. I will take care to speak with feeling about Sacred Scripture, and make myself as familiar with it as possible. The same holds for the Fathers, whom I will quote in Italian so that all can understand. Whenever I am about to preach, I will remind myself that God will demand of me a strict account for all those souls who fail to garner profit from my words; hence I must do all I can to persuade and inspire them to virtue, and to perseverance in it. I will not fuss about style and figures of speech, but when homely stories and allusions help, I will make full use of them, and introduce many examples. As far as possible, I will avoid honourable ministries, such as preaching in cities; and I will be happy to break the bread of the Divine Word to the poor, and peasants and the uneducated.[93]

Whilst there surely are occasions for wit and humour—and Fr Dominic would later agree that there are—the clear thought is that preaching is to be preaching Jesus Christ who has spoken to us in the Sacred Scriptures. 'The less one saw of artifice and studied elegance', recalled one of Fr Dominic's hearers, 'the more one was drawn by a heavenly force that enraptured. In his meditations and conferences, I saw the reflection of a beautiful soul. I was so attracted by him that I revealed to him all the secrets of my soul; in fact, I went back to him a second time, for I had discovered that he was a saint.'[94] Personal piety, zeal and straightforward sincerity were the essence of Fr Dominic's preaching.

10

The English in Rome

TEACHING AND PREACHING ASIDE, Fr Dominic continued in his prayers for England and seeking out opportunities in which he could, to the best of his ability, further the cause of the conversion of England, albeit trying to do so from his monastery in Rome. Rome itself was to provide opportunities for this. English visitors would often be found, having visited the nearby Colosseum and San Gregorio, at the front door of the monastery of Ss John and Paul where Fr Dominic lived. This he saw as a golden opportunity to try to convert them to Catholicism. He went about attempting this with a simple approach that was not particularly well suited to his English guests to whom talking about religion with strangers did not come naturally. Fr Dominic's method involved engaging a lay brother, who himself understood little English, to ask the visitors whether they were Christian or Catholics. If they answered that they were not Catholics, they were then asked what the difference was between a Christian and a Catholic. Whatever the response, the lay brother was then to launch into a short catechesis that concluded by asking whether the visitor wished to receive instruction in the Catholic Faith, there and then. If the visitors showed any interest Fr Dominic was to be called.

It can be imagined that this approach probably yielded little more than astonishment yet there are cases on record that prove its occasional success such as a Scottish gentleman who at first was merely highly amused by the whole performance but yet, as he could not dismiss the lay brother's words, found himself returning a year later with the news that he and all his companions had become Catholics.[95]

A greater boost to Fr Dominic's hopes regarding a mission to England came, as he himself relates in *Arcana Verba*, totally unexpectedly:

> Many years passed without me seeing a single ray of hope of the possibility of my going to England. After about 17 years, I had the occasion to make the acquaintance of Sir Harry Trelawney by being appointed to teach him how to say Mass. He introduced me to Mr Spencer, the latter to Mr Phillipps, and these gentlemen gave me the first inkling of hope that perchance, in the course of time, it might be arranged that I should go to England.[96]

Sir Harry was a recent convert from Cornwall who was preparing to be ordained a priest. Cardinal Carlo Odescalchi (1785–1841), knowing of Fr Dominic's passionate love for England, had suggested that Sir Harry receive instruction on how to say Mass from the holy Passionist. But Fr Dominic's poor English persuaded Sir Harry's daughter, Laetitia, to look elsewhere and, hearing of the arrival in Rome in the spring of 1830 of the Honourable George Spencer, a recent convert himself, she approached Spencer asking him to assist her father.

George Spencer was the youngest son of the Second Earl Spencer and had been an Anglican priest but, in no small part due to the inspiration of the young Ambrose Lisle Phillipps, he had suddenly converted to Catholicism at the beginning of 1830. Both his saddened father and his Vicar Apostolic, Dr Thomas Walsh (1776–1849), thought it best that Spencer should be sent to the English College in Rome for some years to prepare for ordination as a Catholic priest. On his father's part this decision seemed vital as, with a convert's zeal, Spencer was hoping to return to the area of his Anglican parish—the very parish church of his family's country estate—to preach like St Paul against aspects of what he had hitherto taught and bring his flock to the light of the Catholic faith.

By the end of his first year in Rome George Spencer and Fr Dominic had become very good friends, Spencer often visiting Fr Dominic at Ss John and Paul's.

Ambrose Lisle Phillipps was also a convert—shocking his parents with his decision to secretly become a Catholic whilst still at school. Both Phillipps and Spencer were to play a critical role in bringing to fruition Fr Dominic's dream of evangelizing in England. Very soon after having first met, Spencer introduced Fr Dominic to his rector, Mgr Nicholas Wiseman (1802–65), the future first Cardinal Archbishop of Westminster. Spencer and Phillipps were thrilled by the zeal and love for England showed by Fr Dominic and could only attribute it to God's work that such a priest who knew so little of England itself should have such a strong desire for the country's conversion. This was certainly the desire of Spencer, Phillipps and Wiseman, the former two presenting a more optimistic vision of the possible harvest of souls that they thought imminent than was the case to both Fr Dominic and Wiseman.

But Fr Dominic was incredibly excited too: his encounters with these Englishmen were surely divine signs of blessing for the work that he believed that he was called to do. Their hopes confirmed his own recent experiences in prayer.[97] And as his hopes rose and his happiness in the company of his new friends increased, Fr Dominic was sent from Rome to Lucca as the Superior of the new Passionist retreat there.

11

Lucca

L EAVING ROME IN THE SUMMER OF 1831, Fr Dominic was not to know that he would never live
there again. The Retreat to which he was being
sent had been newly built by Duke Charles Louis de
Bourbon in thanksgiving for a miraculous favour
obtained through the intercession of St Paul of the
Cross, then not yet canonized. Whatever the inner
sufferings of his soul, his time as rector of the Retreat
in Lucca was to be one of the happiest times of Fr
Dominic's life and remembered by members of his
community as an era of 'the greatest tranquillity,
peace and good order'.[98]

Part of the reason for the community's contentment with Fr Dominic was that they could see that
he invested his trust in those that he believed worthy.
Fr Augustine, a priest who lived under Fr Dominic's
direction, left a record of a conversation that he had
once had with his superior. Fr Augustine had said
to Fr Dominic,

> 'Whenever I come to your room, you always
> seem miles away, and when I ask for something,
> you invariably say "yes". What would you

do, if one fine day, I requested something that you could not grant?' Dominic replied: 'When anyone comes to my room, I take a quick look to see who he is. If I say "yes" without waiting to hear his request, it is because I am sure that his request will be reasonable and not contrary to virtue. But, if the request comes from one who is not entirely trustworthy, I do not answer "yes" immediately, but wait to see what he wants.'[99]

The contentment of the community spilled over to relations between the Passionists and the local people, civil and ecclesiastical authorities too. This is not to say that Fr Dominic did not impose discipline on those that he believed needed it but, it seems, as well as profiting from his rule, the community was blessed with many of its members having been formed by their superior's very own novice master, Fr Bernard.

Whilst making such a good impression on his confreres, Fr Dominic's heart was still very much directed towards being a missionary in England. Letter after letter of his from this time are extravagant in their longing to travel and settle in 'dear England'.

I should like to hear frequently about the progress that our holy religion makes in that island which is never absent from my poor heart. Ah, who will give me the wings of a dove to fly thither? . . . I rejoice in the hope of being one day able to reach it. Dear England! Beloved Nation! when shall I see thee restored to the loving bosom of our holy Mother the Church? Then I shall be able to say 'Nunc dimittis servum tuum, Domine quia viderunt oculi mei salutare tuum! [Now thou dost dismiss Thy servant, Lord, because my eyes have seen Thy salvation!]' I hope to wait for the time of the divine mercies.[100]

The sweet hope consoles me, which you give me of coming to England to found our Congregation there. Oh, happy day, when will it come? It is true that I am an instrument totally inadequate for so great a work; but God can make use of whosoever He pleases and that is my consolation. Oh, could I but sacrifice my life and give my blood for my beloved brethren of England! I hope that if I do not give my blood, I shall at least exhaust my strength for them.[101]

In 1831 a meditation that he had written in Sant' Angelo entitled *The Lament of England*, a reflection on the Lamentations of Jeremiah that were read during the Holy Week ceremonies, was published by Phillipps in England. For Fr Dominic, these words of the prophet Jeremiah seemed most applicable to the Church in England, an understanding that was indeed shared by the Catholics of England, especially at the time of the Reformation. *The Lament* is not a work of literary merit but, surely due to the sincerity with which it was written and the way in which Fr Dominic identifies himself with English Catholics, it greatly moved St John Henry Newman when he read it. 'Lord,' wrote Fr Dominic,

if faith, nay if reason itself, did not assure me that You never forget anyone, and that You see and care for all, I should be tempted to become blasphemous and assert that You must have forgotten Your servants, the people of England.

> Lord, how can You witness our numberless miseries and not take pity on us?

Fr Dominic continues,

> We have sinned, it is true, but that does not mean that You have lost Your sovereign rights over us. Have the floods of our iniquities extinguished the furnace of Your love for us? ... Are our sins greater than Your mercy?

Fr Dominic begs God to relent and have mercy on England, restoring her ancient heritage for the sake of

> Augustine, Dunstan, Edmund, Anselm, Thomas of Canterbury, Hugh of Lincoln, Chad of Lichfield, Swithyn of Winchester, and innumerable other saints ... who lift up their grieving hands to the throne of the Divine Majesty.

The Lament is certainly not a document imbued with ecumenism but it still stands as a powerful prayer from one who, as Alfred Wilson notes, 'felt no need to be on his best behaviour in the Divine Presence. He pleaded with God as he would have pleaded with a fellow man, because he knew from personal experience that "Jesus is more human than humanity".'[102] Even though he was still firmly ensconced in Italy, Fr Dominic was already beginning to influence Catholics in England: Spencer and Phillipps, with whom he kept up contact, were soon to take up his and his order's founder's campaign of encouraging prayers for the conversion of England.

Two further responsibilities were given to Fr Dominic during 1832 and 1833 when he was appointed as the second of two advisers to the Passionist Provincial and as professor of sacred eloquence for the newly ordained priests. The first role gave him the opportunity to speak at the General Chapter of 1833, pleading for the opening of a Passionist mission to England. He failed to convince the members of the Chapter but, rather than outrightly rejecting the idea, they deferred further deliberation until the next General Chapter in 1839. He took his second role as seriously as can be expected rising at 3am every morning to spend two hours each day preparing a specimen sermon for his class. The effort that he expended on this work saw him enlarge his volumes of sermon notes to 8,000 folio pages before finally admitting that, as far as fresh ideas from him went, he had 'emptied his shop'.[103]

On 12 December 1831, at Pieve di Moriano, Fr Dominic preached his first mission, a ministry that was to become a substantial part of his vocation for the rest of his life. As one priest was to attest of one such mission, 'I could never have believed that so much good could have been done in so short a time'.[104] He continued to write, sometimes seeking to refute errant teaching on church doctrine, one such volume of 262 pages proffering a vision of Christian society being praised by the Reader of the Congregation of Rites as 'vast and well-marshalled erudition; acute, forceful and lively reasoning; as well as urbanity and respect for his adversary'.[105]

Another work from this period are three volumes of apologetics which grew from Fr Dominic's discussions and correspondence with an Anglican clergyman, the Rev'd Mr Ford. Within this work Fr Dominic developed and set out his understanding of the reality of papal infallibility, writings which, according to Pope St Paul VI, 'anticipates with the secure appraisal of scholarship, the definition which was to be made many years later by the First Vatican Council'.[106] Fr Dominic was assisted in his setting out of the apologetics by a list of Protestant objections to Catholic doctrine that was supplied by George Spencer. The Reader from the Congregation of Rites, during the beatification process, heaped further praise on this work:

> A splendid and compact apologia ... pregnant with sane and amiable doctrine ... truly a golden little tract ... 46 pages of solid doctrine, sound common-sense and heart-warming undertones ... his treatment of the dispute about the efficacy of Grace is outstanding and deserves to be published and amplified ... written vivaciously and with magisterial ease ... a model Catholic apologetic, competent, well-informed, profound and pleasing.[107]

During Fr Dominic's lifetime, however, such praise as he received for his academic efforts was more than eclipsed by suspicion and condemnation. His response, when teaching in Rome, to the popular writings of the philosopher and political theorist Felicite de Lamennais (1782–1854) earned him the rebuke of his confreres and superiors. Only following the condemnation of Lamennais's errors by the Holy See in 1833 was this particular cloud of opprobrium lifted from over him. But his reputation was still not fully restored as his three volume *Course of Philosophy for Passionist Students*, also written in Rome, was condemned as allegedly unfaithful to the teaching of St Thomas Aquinas and, in consequence, unsuitable for Passionists. The censors who had been engaged to examine Fr Dominic's work all seem to have been in some way or other favourable to the works of Lamennais. To the General's strongly worded letter communicating to Fr Dominic the censors' condemnation, Fr Dominic decided to write a detailed defence. He placed his response on Our Lady's Altar and prayed for some hours after which he burned his defence, writing instead to the General humbly asking him to ask those whom he had taught regarding his faithfulness to Thomistic principles. Of this work, like so many others written by Fr Dominic, the Reader from the Congregation of Rites was fulsome in his praise.[108] The ban of publishing his philosophy course was eventually lifted in 1833 when Fr Dominic became Provincial of the southern Italian Province but by that time he had no time to prepare it for publication.

There can be no doubt that the rejection of his work, with the added sting that he might not be a good Passionist for having written works that were suspected or condemned, came as a tremendous shock to Fr Dominic. Yet he brought all this to prayer as best as he could, as his diary records:

> Every day I will ask for this grace, among others, to suffer for love of Jesus Christ, and to be

humiliated, despised and belittled for love of Him. God has given me great graces this year, especially by sending me many humiliations. I must be very grateful to Our Lord for having condescended to humble my pride. My God, treat me always like this. Humble me as You please, and in whatever way You please, provided I can bear it without offending You.[109]

12

Provincial 1833–1836

THAT HIS FELLOW PASSIONISTS voted for Fr Dominic to become their Provincial clearly indicates that they valued him and the way that he was guiding the community at Lucca. Fr Dominic himself did not underestimate the task that lay ahead of him and so, as was his wont, he set down resolutions for the future:

> From now onwards, along with St Paul of the Cross, I will take St Francis de Sales as my co-model in government, and strive to keep his example in mind always, and to the best of my ability, imitate it.
>
> I must make a special effort to emulate him in meekness and courtesy and every day ask him to obtain these virtues for me. As far as possible, I will read some of his writings every day, especially his letters.
>
> I will strive to keep calm; and if I am ruffled, I will maintain silence and not make decisions; and if by any mischance I do break into speech then, I will penance myself and make reparation.
>
> I will never correct anyone unless I feel at peace with myself; and before starting to correct, I will always say at least one Hail Mary.

I will always be on my guard never to use expressions that are insulting or humiliating.

I will avoid as a pest any partiality in the display of affection, and treat all alike.

I will be careful not to mention anything that discredits another religious, especially in the presence of one who ought not to know about it; and if I am forced to speak, I will exercise the greatest moderation.

In important matters, I will never make a decision without first seeking advice from those most competent to give it.

I will be careful never to censure the conduct of major superiors, even if it is blameworthy.

I will never speak, and much less write, one single syllable about the various theories with regard to God's part in human acts, etc, and I will keep to this, even if I am provoked. I will be even more careful never by word or writing to censure those who disagree with me.

I will take care to be always cheerful, especially during recreation and when interviewing others.

I will never post a letter without first re-reading it in cold blood.

I will read good books on the art of ruling, especially those which discuss the methods of ruling of the saints.

I will read carefully, and often, the decrees of Chapters, the encyclicals, the Regulations.

On missions, I will do everything possible to avoid making changes without necessity.

I will attend, as far as possible, to the study of canon law.

I will make myself all things to all men to gain all for Christ. Amen.[110]

On becoming Provincial, Fr Dominic returned to

live in Paliano. Perhaps remembering that when he himself first arrived there as a novice that there was no room for him in the novitiate, one of his first acts was to enlarge the novitiate building. He actively promoted Passionist missions in the province giving as many himself as priests for whom giving missions was their sole responsibility. He also prepared the young priests to give missions.

Very soon after arriving at Paliano Fr Dominic made a visitation of the five Passionist houses that were under his jurisdiction. At this time, and subsequently, he interacted with his brethren in a kindly and paternal way, not looking for opportunities for corrections or laying down new minor rules, as others might do. Instead, typically, he would simply write in the Retreat's register words such as 'As I found nothing out of order that could not be dealt with privately, I made no decrees and contented myself at the closing with urging the brethren to exact observance of the Rules and Regulations, and then completed the usual ceremonies'.[111]

As Provincial, Fr Dominic's humility made him 'believe in practice that he was not the superior'[112] — he 'ruled more by affability and kindness than by command'.[113] He was as approachable as he always had been and insisted on carrying out tasks around the Retreat that normally superiors left to others. As a student Fr Dominic had noted in his diary, 'In these days I have had practical experience of the immense harm that results from the excessive severity of a superior, and to what hazards it exposes the virtue of subjects'. The 'excessive severity of a superior', he wrote, 'is generally the cause of the complete ruination of subjects.' There follow various resolutions that he would follow if ever he 'should have the misfortune to be a superior'. At first reading resolutions such as 'I must be affable to all, especially to the weak, and put up with their shortcomings like a father' are clearly very worthy but perhaps read a little like the promises many a father makes before his children grow up and become more challenging. Still, it seems that by and large Fr Dominic really did live by the resolutions that he made as a student: 'I will take as my standard the meekness and gentleness of Jesus Christ, as well as that of St Francis de Sales, and of St Vincent de Paul … To all, I will do all the good that I can.'[114]

Given the aspiration to be a gentle guide of souls it was still possible for Fr Dominic to be very firm when matters of the Passionist rule of life were failing to be observed. One of the rectors of his province records

> I held Fr Dominic in great esteem because I never could discover in him even a trace of duplicity or insincerity, or the least adulteration of human prudence. He spoke as he felt and thought, never caring whether what he said would turn to his advantage or disadvantage. Provided what he said was in conformity with truth and justice, he was satisfied.[115]

Throughout his years as Provincial Fr Dominic continued to write. One work of 260 pages, *The Dialogue of Fraternal Charity*, that was written at the request of nuns, refers to three other works, all of which are now lost. Sickness also marked his time as Provincial, an inflammatory illness being so bad at the beginning of 1834 that he was expected to die from loss of blood and received the Last Rites, though he believed that he would not die as he had not yet set foot in England.

Also attributed to Fr Dominic at this time were exceptional spiritual gifts. Along with receiving visions of Our Lady the thought of her could send him into ecstasy. One account, given by a Passionist Father, Gaetano of the Heart of Jesus, recalled when, the day before his final profession, he was being interviewed by Fr Dominic. Just as he was about to leave Fr Dominic gestured towards a picture of the Blessed Virgin Mary, exhorting the novice to real love of her. Suddenly he fell silent and his face became radiant with light as he was raised from the floor, floating in the air before beginning to speak again. Unsurprisingly from that day onwards the novice 'venerated Fr Dominic as a saint and intense lover of Mary, and could never recall that incident without being moved to devotion to both Our Lady and to Fr Dominic'.[116]

✣ 13 ✣

Cholera

A T THE PROVINCIAL CHAPTER OF 1836 Fr Dominic was elected first consultor to his successor as provincial. He moved from Paliano to the retreat at S. Sosio and, being freed of the office of provincial, he filled much of his time by giving missions.

In early 1837 cholera broke out at Ceprano, a small town nearby. Eighty of the residents, victims of the disease, were thrown out of the town and herded into poorly constructed shacks nearby where they received little assistance from anyone. The local authority asked the Passionists of S. Sosio to send a priest to minister to these people. The whole community volunteered so lots were cast and Fr Dominic, who as a consultor of the provincial could have easily excused himself from volunteering, was chosen as the priest to be sent. He immediately set off having packed just a bible, breviary and writing materials. Yet he did not receive a warm welcome in Ceprano from either local clergy or an anti-clerical group led by two agnostic doctors.

All the main churches of the town had been closed to prevent people from gathering together in large numbers and the contagion spreading so Fr Dominic was given care of a small church dedicated to St Francis that was on the outskirts of the town. In his eagerness to go to Ceprano there had been no time to arrange accommodation for him and due to the perceived danger of disease many families whom he approached refused to give him a lodging. Eventually he found someone, Signore Roccantonio Celletti, who was willing to offer him hospitality. He was shown to a large room in the house but asked for the smallest one instead. He was going to have little need of the room beyond sleeping as he was constantly on the move making his way through the streets of Ceprano, visiting the sick and the dying. Constantly a cheerful presence he became known as the 'Liberating Angel',[117] ministering day and night remaining with the dying until they drew their last breath. If there was any spare time, he spent it in the church praying or in his room writing. Sometimes the sound of Fr Dominic scourging himself could be heard from his room—the occupant of the neighbouring room would hear his alarm go off in the middle of the night awakening Fr Dominic to prayer. The Celletti family were able to observe their guest's rule of life: he would only go for short walks on the evening of feast days; he would eat only one proper meal each day. He would prepare at length to celebrate Mass and spent a long time in thanksgiving afterwards. He would frequently visit the Blessed Sacrament and, if he were free, he would spend hours in prayer in the church in the evening. He would hear Confessions for as long as necessary—and still he would write, working on the second part of his commentary on the Song of Songs as well as a refutation of a tract that the two agnostic doctors already mentioned had produced.

His host at Ceprano became understandably concerned that her family might be infected by their immensely active guest, but Fr Dominic assured them, as he was to assure a doctor of the town, that they would remain in perfect health, as indeed they did. In the same spirit he promised some victims for whom all hope was lost that they would recover, and they did. More miraculous yet, he would turn up at deathbeds only seconds after having attended another, sometimes without even being summoned there. He also knew when victims had died even though he was not present at their deathbed and could not have heard the news from anyone else.

Other extraordinary powers were also ascribed to him. He was able to direct one family to the whereabouts of a vital document that they had lost; he warned a young man that he must go to Confession immediately, the man dying three days later; he was able to tell penitents their sins if they became too tongue-tied to do so themselves. 'Whilst he was in my house', his hostess later recalled, 'I venerated him as a saint and often invoked him, and always successfully.'[118]

Although he did not succumb to the plague, Fr Dominic's health suffered from the continual strain that the work he carried out imposed on his body.

He neglected a feverish cold and began to suffer excruciating heartburns that would double him up in pain. At first it was feared that he too had fallen ill with the cholera and no one would assist him. The illness left him with a weakness in his legs for the remainder of his life, making it impossible for him to mount a horse without the help of others.

When the cholera abated, having thanked his hostess, Fr Dominic quietly slipped back to S. Sosio. As well as giving missions he continued his writing including completing a 1,872-page course of moral theology, a short tract on the question of God's part in human acts, a volume entitled *The Spotless Parish Priest* that includes a riposte to Jansenism, a book for nuns that he called *The Divine Paranymph, Dialogues of Prayer* and more. Ill-health increasingly dogged him yet his love for England remained constant, as was his hope that he would be sent there: the former an ever-present reality, the latter seeming to be a vanishing dream.

✤ 14 ✤

'For Christ I am a legate'

I N AN EXCELLENT INTRODUCTION to the subject of miracles in the life of Fr Dominic, Alfred Wilson notes that saints are canonized 'because they practised heroic virtue … Not because they worked wonders'. 'Extraordinary gifts may confirm, but they do not constitute, sanctity.' Evidence is all important. If in the past miracles in lives of the saints sometimes were 'multiplied uncritically', this led to 'uncritical omission of all marvels'. Ultimately, 'Scepticism is no more objective than credulity'. Wilson goes on to state that with regard to the miraculous in Fr Dominic's apostolate, 'For the facts reported, there is much — and often far more — evidence than there is for facts recorded as certain in secular history books'. He cites reliable witnesses who gave their testimonies under oath, testimonies that were then subjected to critical examination by others along with evidence that the miracles in question did not undermine the humility and obedience of the one through whose hands the miracles were worked. 'Marvels are assumed to be susceptible of a natural explanation until the contrary is demonstrated.'[119]

The 'marvels' recorded of Fr Dominic are many. One such took place in the sight of the whole community of Poor Clares at Anagni. Whilst Fr Dominic was saying Mass, he was transfigured in a Pentecostal light which seemed to stream from heaven. Fr Dominic's own autobiography recalls of the visit merely that 'When I was at Anagni acting as occasional confessor for the Poor Clares, God gave me the strongest impulses always to concern myself about His glory'.[120]

There are various accounts of Fr Dominic being transfixed in ecstasy whilst in prayer. The handyman at the same Poor Clare convent just mentioned once saw, late one night, what seemed like an incandescent halo hovering above the room where Fr Dominic was staying. In case it was a fire, the handyman went to investigate, knocking on the retreat giver's door with increasing insistence but receiving no response. Finally, he opened the door to see Fr Dominic as still as a statue. The handyman thought that the Father was ill, perhaps paralysed, so he banged the table, shouted, and then shook the priest, all to no avail. Perhaps a little afraid and certainly perplexed the handyman returned to his own room and was greatly relieved when he saw Fr Dominic up and about the following day.

Such ecstasies were not uncommon for Fr Dominic, particularly when preaching retreats. The gift of prophecy was also an abundant charism for him. One example from many comes from the end of a retreat that he had given at the Benedictine convent of Bauco. As he was preparing to leave, the servant, Agnes Botticelli, came to him for his blessing. Noticing that she was weeping Fr Dominic said to her, 'Don't weep, child, you will be married soon and your first child will be a boy, who will become a Passionist and be named Dominic of the Heart of Mary, but he will never say Mass'. As foretold, the young lady soon married and her firstborn son became a Passionist and was known as Confrater Dominic of the Heart of Mary, being a sub-deacon when he died of tuberculosis at the retreat of Moricone.[121]

Accounts of bi-location and miracles of multiplying food and healing the sick also are recorded. The effect on Fr Dominic himself seems to be that his humility and his compassion increased, as did his use of humour in talks such as this example from one talk that he gave on the examination of conscience:

> One comes across certain priests who are just bone-lazy. To gain exemption from work they dedicate themselves to mysticism, or to put it bluntly, to humbug. They are men of prayer, of study, of reading, even of indispositions, but of the sort of indispositions that only those who suffer them can understand. Maybe their indispositions are produced by superior forces unknown to Galen! This being the case, with their affected devotion they easily secure exemption from the more exacting choir-observances, such as getting up for midnight Mattins. In the morning they rise to make their prayer, and after prayer there is the Way of the Cross; then a little coffee is called for—or even chocolate—it's good for the stomach, you

know. And with all this palaver we come to
mid-morning. You might fancy that they would
then do some work. You are mistaken. This
morning in prayer they received ... they must
get advice because ... They trot off to their
spiritual father and recount their ecstasies, their
amorous swoons, or to be brief, the ravings of
their crazy fantasy. Alas, if they find a director
of the same kidney! That clinches it; then neither
the father studies nor the son works. The
spiritual conference goes on until the hours of
Sext and None. Then the director goes to choir,
and the directed to stretch his legs and work
up an appetite and you can rest assured that
he will do credit to the cook and the cellarer.
Botheration! Beans again, though they cause
flatulence and disturb the spirit's operations!
A chicken a day would be needed for them,
and I assure you that if any such unfortunate
fowl ever falls under those devout nails it will
not even escape with its bones. He sets about
it with such great devotion that you would be
tempted to think that he is contemplating the
divine attributes in it. He eviscerates it, strips
the bones, studies the joints and, to savour
better the divine sanctity in it, sucks even the
tiniest bones until there are no pickings left
for the unfortunate cat. After dinner there are
dishes to wash, but his hands tremble. These
mystical allurements! He breaks everything
he touches. Better to go up and refresh the
spirit and give some salutary advice to those
benighted, dissipated fellows across there. He
is hardly there, and if you heard the panaceas
that he comes out with, you might fancy him
the most expert quack who ever existed. Alas
for certain dreams! ... Purgations of the spirit,

of course; he is suffering the passive purgations. He must consult St Theresa and St John of the Cross, and before the consultations are over it is night time. Why doesn't he do some work? You are naïve. Mary has chosen the better part which shall not be taken away from her.[122]

By way of contrast his remarks could also be totally sober if necessary, such as when speaking to senior priests of the order during a Chapter:

> A superior must supply what remedies he can for human weakness. Even the rod? What do you want me to say? I know Moses used a rod on the Egyptians, but he used it very sparingly in Israel, and once when he did use it, it was to produce flowers.[123]

In a work of 1837 *Apparato all'apostolico ministero* (116 pages intended for Passionist communities) Fr Dominic addresses many issues that faced priests then, and now. 'Beware of the bombastic grandiloquence and studied obscurantism of certain would-be, up-to-date writers', he warned, 'Anyone who raises his voice against them is at once shouted down and informed that he has failed to grasp their meaning.' This could lead to the censurer being 'dismissed as an idiot', 'And so, because they are scared of being classified as stupid, many are afraid to raise their voices, and in order to pass as intelligent pretend to have understood the author perfectly'.[124] Prophets of doom, those who use invective, harshness, sweeping statements or wholesale condemnations to attempt to achieve their ends are asked

Is it wise to scare people like that? All I know is that most sinners are not converted by it. In fact, it only serves to convince them that all is lost. Would it not be wiser to open their hearts to hope? They do not deserve to be manhandled like that.[125]

The pulpit is not the place for discussions of controversial questions of theology. Of course the people need instruction, but instruction in what? In Thomism? In Molinism? Not at all. All they seek is knowledge of how to sanctify themselves, or at least of how to save their souls, and for that it is not necessary to be either a Thomist or a Molinist, but only a good Christian. When I address my students, I am aware that I am a Thomist; but when I preach to ordinary people, I forget all about that, and all I remember is that I am a Catholic. For Christ I am a legate, not for Thomism, nor for any other party interest.[126]

Throughout the *Apparato all'apostolico ministero* Fr Dominic exhorts his readers to study more and to use scriptural passages more frequently in sermons:

Sin is not eradicated by Greek or Roman eloquence, but by the word of God, which is the only sword capable of exercising sin from souls ... I would never approve of anyone attempting to preach unless he has first read and mastered the holy bible ... It is absolutely untrue that all are familiar with the texts and facts of Scripture ... To whom do we preach? To the people. And do the Italian people read Scripture? I should be happy if even the clergy read it, but many of them never get further than the covers. They read newspapers, poetic fables, comedies and

novels, but leave the Bible in a corner. And so
the facts and texts of scripture are new to almost
everybody, and this is all the more true because
modern preachers (whether from ignorance or
anxiety to be fashionable, I know not) seldom
deign to quote it.[127]

Fr Dominic usually wrote under obedience, being
asked by others to consider various aspects of the
Faith, be it dogma, morals, or piety. What happened
next to his work seems not to have much troubled
him at all. In the preface to his *Marialogy* he wrote,

I have no intention of publishing what I am
going to write. Why then write, someone will
ask, why sprawl ink across paper which will
serve only to encumber a corner of an old library,
or maybe torn up and thrown into the fire? Well
then, I intend to write even though what I write
will be of no use to others. These writings will at
least be useful to me, and perhaps they may even
be useful to one or two of my religious brethren.
By the time they crumble into dust, they may
perhaps have been useful to someone who
had leisure to read them. Even if it is decided
to tear them up and throw them into the fire, I
can at least rejoice that they have suffered the
fate that I myself deserved.[128]

✥ 15 ✥

Towards England

B Y 1838 THE PASSIONISTS were considering the possibility of three new foundations: one at Boulogne, one at Tournai and another in England. The last of these proposals was being actively supported by Spencer, his cousin Mrs Canning and Monsignor Charles Acton, auditor of the Apostolic Chamber and future cardinal. At first the prospects for the project to succeed seemed good and with the election of Fr Dominic's former spiritual director, Fr Anthony of St James, as General of the order the outcome looked certain. But it was not to be as practical support that had previously been offered by Phillipps, Spencer and Mrs Canning crumbled away.

To make matters worse for Fr Dominic, he was then re-elected provincial of his own province. With his ever-failing health it looked as if he was never going to minister in England. He wrote to the General,

> Today marks the end of 26 years and 3 months of waiting for this grace, but I can go on waiting as long again if God gives me life, without losing one iota of the certainty I have had from the beginning. I recognize that I am full of

infirmities, crippled with ailments, unable to walk and even less able to ride a horse; however, even if my disabilities were to increase tenfold, I would still not lose hope because 'He who has promised is powerful and able to fulfil'. My only fear is that God may be forced to retract His promises because of my pride. I derive comfort, however, from the thought that 'the gifts of God are without repentance'.[129]

The foundation at Tournai, however, was planned to go ahead and, at first, Fr Dominic's name was on the list of those named to go there, probably being named superior of the new house. But he was not among those appointed to go. Disappointed though he was he did not doubt that ultimately the Passionists would not set out to Belgium without him: 'You will see, I shall be sent', he told his confreres.[130] One day as he was passing a wayside shrine to Our Lady with fellow Passionists, asking them to pray that he might go to 'Tournai e non tourne . . .' ('Tournai and not return').[131]

By the middle of April 1840, the situation had not changed, and Fr Dominic had returned to San Sosio to recuperate after giving a mission and recover from an infection which was causing him great discomfort. One of the Passionists was at his bedside visiting him and discussing with him the news about the Belgian mission. Fr Dominic's reaction greatly surprised him:

He spoke as if he were a robust man and already selected for the mission, and his words and gestures were so animated with

zeal that I was surprised. What surprised
me most was the strength of his conviction
that he would end his days in England,
though everything then seemed to point to
the contrary. I concluded that he must have
received a revelation from heaven.

As the two were talking a letter for Fr Dominic from
the Passionist General arrived: 'I noticed him smile
as he read it and took it for granted that it contained
the good news of his selection for the mission.' It was
exactly the opposite—a delayed communication that
informed him that others had been chosen instead.
But, smiling, Fr Dominic then said to his visitor, 'I
suppose I ought to be upset but this list won't do.
Our Lady has revealed that one of these four will
accompany me to England. How comes it then that
he is on the list, and I am not? The General will
change his mind.'[132] The very next day Fr Dominic
received a letter confirming his belief and, having
sought the approval of his confessor for the appoint-
ment, he set out for Rome the following morning.

Accounts of his departing San Sosio record that,
apart from his confessor, his confreres tried to persuade him not to leave. Their concern for him was
confirmed as they witnessed the spasms of pain that
shot through him as he was helped to mount his
horse and as they accompanied him, supporting him
on both sides, as he began his journey. At Ceprano,
thanks to arrangements made by his confessor, Fr
Dominic was transferred to a carriage, arriving in
Rome on 14 May.

On the day before his departure, the Father General of the Passionists brought Fr Dominic and his three companions who were to travel to Tournai—Frs Seraphim and Peter, and Br Crispin—to the Vatican to receive the blessing of Pope Gregory XVI (1765–1846). The pope and Fr Dominic already knew each other as when the pope had been a monk at the neighbouring monastery of S Gregory on the Caelian Hill he had sought the assistance of Fr Dominic in seeking out tomes in the library of Ss John and Paul.

Having made one last visit to the tomb of St Paul of the Cross, Fr Dominic and his companions set out on their mission: it was the Feast of Our Lady Help of Christians. From Rome they went to Citavecchia, continuing by steamer to Marseilles where they were greeted by St Eugène de Mazenod (1782–1861), founder of the Oblates of Mary Immaculate, who paid for their tickets for their journey to Lyons. On 12 June the holy companions arrived at Ere in Belgium, to establish the first Passionist foundation outside of Italy.

16

Ere

T HE HOUSE that was to become the Passionist Retreat at Ere was, Fr Dominic considered, much more suited to its new purpose than he had expected but it was completely bereft of furnishings and the kitchen had no utensils whatsoever. Fr Dominic's first concern was to establish a chapel and, a little over a month after having arrived, his new community was able to celebrate Mass and reserve the Blessed Sacrament in the newly created chapel. This was only possible once the local bishop had inspected the chapel himself. Likewise, the bishop examined Fr Dominic and his companions as to their knowledge of moral theology before granting them the necessary faculties to hear Confessions.

On the Feast of Our Lady of Mount Carmel, 16 July, the community began the customary night and day choir-observance of the Passionists. As often happens when good works proceed, Fr Dominic and his companions were almost immediately subjected to malicious gossip and slander, it being rumoured that they had been expelled from Italy in disgrace and were merely parasitical beggars, bleeding other local churches of funds. Fr Dominic rejoiced in these calumnies seeing them as a clear sign of Satan's anger at their work. 'Contradictions, accusations and calumny', he wrote to the General, 'are the true and stable foundations of religious houses. I praise God for deeming us worthy to suffer something for Him.' [133]

Not only did Fr Dominic not attempt to defend his community's good reputation but neither did he go about founding the house in the way that almost everyone else would have recommended. His approach was 'to ask for nothing from anyone; to go out from the retreat as little as possible; not to enter any house in the neighbourhood; to persevere in prayer and give good example in all things'.[134] His only regret was that he could not help his confrere, Br Crispin, who was clearly dying, aged only 26.

Having become proficient in French, Fr Dominic began to take up the role of giving retreats to clergy, seminarians and religious communities as he had already done for much of his life. He became good friends with the rector of the seminary in Tournai not only giving three retreats there and preaching often during his time in Belgium but also, at the rector's request, writing a manual of canon law for the students along with various tracts on subjects of moral theology and a 'directory' of guidance for the rector himself. Likewise, the Bishop of Tournai, having at first been rather cold towards his newest religious community, invited Fr Dominic to preach in the cathedral, offered him the role of Diocesan censor and presented the Passionist retreat with a silver chalice. Very quickly the Passionists established the esteem of the local community, the internuncio at Brussels writing to the Passionist General saying that

> My patronage is really quite unnecessary, because the excellent religious that you have sent here are their own recommendation. Their exalted virtue and golden simplicity have won the admiration of all ... The Bishop of Tournai has assured me that they have nothing to fear because they have already won everybody's affection.[135]

Despite all the good that was that initial Passionist community, it attracted very few men who persevered in their vocations. This cross was lightened for Fr Dominic when, in August 1841, the General sent him four Italian priests and a brother to augment the community. Perhaps the General's confidence in the prospects of the retreat at Ere had been bolstered not just by the good reports that he received of the community but also by the owner of the house where the Passionists had settled deciding to donate the building to the order in July 1841.

17

First Visit to England

EANWHILE IN ROME the prospects for Fr Dominic to realize his lifelong desire were increasing. Between 28 May and 4 June 1840 Mgr Nicholas Wiseman had chosen to make the retreat before his episcopal consecration at the motherhouse of the Passionists, Ss John and Paul, in Rome and among his first acts as co-adjutor to Bishop Walsh of the Midland District was to seek out a place where Fr Dominic could establish a Passionist community. From Oscott, where Bishop Wiseman had also been installed as rector, he wrote to Fr Dominic in Ere:

> If on my way through Belgium I did not visit you, it was not for want of time, but only from my having heard, from a French priest who had come from Tournai, that one of your community, whom I naturally concluded to be your paternity, was already in England. I hoped to find you here, but have been disappointed. It seems to me that the moment of your coming to England is not far distant. Our good Bishop, Monsignor Walsh, has already fixed eyes on the house and mission at

Aston Hall, situated in the country, and not far
from the residence of the Earl of Shrewsbury. It
was formerly a convent of nuns and afterwards
a Franciscan house and is therefore well suited
for the purpose of a religious community.
There is annexed to it an extensive piece of
ground (which may yield at the rate of £40
per year) fit for the pasture of cows, where the
country people make great use of milk; and
moreover, there is an annual stipend of about
£80 for the support of the church and mission.
The house with its garden, is surrounded by a
moat, which can be filled with running water,
so that it is a perfect retreat. The only difficulty
which I foresee regards the service of the
parish, since it is necessary that there should
be instructions given and Confessions heard
in English. In the circumstances, however, I
recommend to your paternity to write on the
subject to the Most Rev. Father General, to
obtain his permission for you to come and
examine everything; and if you think fit, you
may forward this letter of mine.[136]

And so, in November 1840, Fr Dominic travelled
to England. 'When I came to Boulogne and went to
say my prayers,' he wrote to the General, 'I received
great favours from the Lord; but was told at the same
time that I should be prepared to suffer great tribulations, the nature of which was not revealed to me.'
The first of these tribulations soon became apparent
as Fr Dominic continues by saying that 'Just at this
time a letter was put into my hand from Mr Spencer,
advising me not to go to England now as the time
was not favourable for doing anything.'[137] Spencer

was to be proven right. Still, after prayer and after consulting with a confessor, he decided to continue on his journey, seeing the coast of England for the first time from the heights of the Cathedral of Notre Dame that was then being built at Boulogne.

Once landed in England, Fr Dominic travelled up to London and then onwards to Birmingham and Oscott where he was greeted warmly by Wiseman and Spencer but rather coldly by the rest of the staff there. He immediately discovered that the owner of Aston Hall had decided not to sell the property after all, thus it was not advisable at that time to look over the house. After three weeks Fr Dominic returned home, breaking his journey briefly to spend a weekend with Phillipps and his family at Grace-Dieu. Apart from his fare, the journey cost 3 pence: 2 pence was the cost of a pork pie in London and 1 penny the cost of some bread. He drank water from public fountains and otherwise neither ate nor drank until he arrived, undoubtedly very hungry and tired, at Ere.

His short English sojourn gave Fr Dominic a useful new, and more realistic, perspective on the country than he had received from Spencer or Phillipps. But this new perspective was no less faith-filled and hopeful for that. Straight away he wrote a long and detailed report for the General that enumerated all the positive developments that he had witnessed in the Midlands: new churches being opened and parishes being established and the developments within the Tractarian movement being among the areas that most excited him.

Returning to Ere, Fr Dominic was also returning to the issue of a lack of vocations, an issue not made easier by the rigidity of the novice master, Fr Seraphim. Fr Seraphim was clearly of a quite different temperament to Fr Dominic, the former introverted, reserved and fastidious, the latter impulsive, intuitive and warm-hearted. Fr Dominic believed that it was both necessary and possible to adapt some of the distinctly Italian customs of the order to the culture of northern Europe. If Fr Seraphim agreed in principle, it seems that he did not really agree in practice and with increasing regularity wrote to the General to complain about the way his superior was governing the retreat. These letters received a hearing in Rome for the General wrote to Fr Dominic criticizing his conduct. A chastened Fr Dominic responded to the General, writing 'On my knees I beg pardon for any displeasure I may have caused you since I came here'.[138]

Some years later Fr Seraphim was appointed Secretary-General of the Passionists and thus had in his possession the very letters of complaint that he had written about Fr Dominic during their time together. To the letters he added a note:

> Although I am affirming these weaknesses of our Fr Dominic of the Mother of God, I have no intention of derogating in the least from the reality of his sanctity, well-known to me, because I am well aware that even in some of the greatest saints to whom we now give the honours of the Altar, God left certain slight weaknesses, for the providential purpose of thereby preserving

their humility and increasing their holiness . . . I have had the occasion to admire the heroism of his virtue, and he has had even more reason to recognise my wretched nature, which perhaps I have not sufficiently mortified, and which more than once gave him occasion to exercise virtue in an heroic degree, and must have caused him great pain. I ask his pardon and hope that he will pray for me.[139]

As for the possibilities of an English foundation, although he had promised to further the plan, it seemed that Wiseman was doing nothing. To complicate matters further, there came an offer from Scotland, with a choice of three different sites. Fr Dominic was clear that he was called to minister in England but was not against the offer. Then, on 3 July 1841, Fr Dominic received a letter from Spencer informing him that Wiseman was to be in Belgium in three weeks' time. On 2 August Fr Dominic received a note from Wiseman inviting him to meet at the Internunciature in Brussels on the following Friday. After the meeting Fr Dominic wrote to the General:

Msg. Wiseman's desire is that we should set up a novitiate house over there, so that the 'observance' in its entirety can kept, as in Rome. This, he says, will give great edification, especially to the Oxford men, who are well disposed towards us. I am of the same opinion. The Nuncio opposed my departure from Belgium, and decidedly wanted me to stay here, but Msg. Wiseman reacted vigorously. 'Father Dominic must come to England' were his words . . . There was a heated argument about the matter, which I calmed by reminding the Nuncio that England was really the final objective that we had in view when we came to Belgium, and that others would come in my place.[140]

After little more than one year's work in Belgium, Fr Dominic was to leave an indelible impression of his personal sanctity. Writing shortly after his beatification Alfred Wilson noted that 'The sanctity of his period in Belgium is the best attested of the entire processes [of beatification]'.[141] Fr Dominic was to return there frequently, usually at least once a year, for the purposes of visitation of the Passionist houses.

✢ 18 ✢

England

'T HE Second Spring in England', wrote the Jesuit historian Fr James Brodrick, 'did not begin when Newman was converted nor when the Hierarchy was restored. It began on a bleak October day of 1841, when a little Italian priest in comical attire shuffled down a ship's gangway at Folkestone.' Given 28 years devotion to the received inner conviction that he had been called to serve in England and after so many struggles before getting there, it can only be imagined how the frail Fr Dominic felt on that 5 October.

And what a sight this papist priest must have seemed to any who noticed him as he stepped ashore:

> He looked very passable in the habit. He was not handsome, nor was he tall. He was short, and rather stout of body, and his voice was squeaky, but he had an eagle eye, picked up English wonderfully, and could blend sarcasm and irony in the most simple and apparently harmless observation. In secular clothes he was a holy show. His coat was not made in any style known to English tailors; it was neither clerical nor secular; it fitted nowhere; and where it

might fit it was wrongly buttoned. [Actually it was made of habit cloth by the Brother Tailor at Ere, who was innocent of the art of making secular suits. Later he acquired a more becoming one.] He carried a watch when he travelled which might well have served for a town clock amongst the Lilliputians, and required to be arranged every five weeks at least. His waist-coat seemed the cast-off garment of some itinerant hawker, and his pantaloons were evidently constructed without consideration for the length or circumference of the legs they enclosed. His shoes might have done service in the ark of Noah, so ancient, patched, and innocent of polish did they look. To crown all, he wore the meanest and most wretched hat that could be seen in England, out of the collieries. His gait was shuffling, his countenance appeared to be grieving, and was often unshaven. The comical twinkle of his eye when he told a good story, and his grave demeanour when he spoke of heaven, made him seem a compound of all that was humble and sublime in human nature. When he came to see us in recreation he amused us immensely. When we went to him to confession, or to have our vocations decided, we came away in admiration. Altogether, his appearance was so far from elegant that the students called him 'Paddy-Whack' amongst themselves. He possessed marvellous sway over us all, and could do what he liked with us.[142]

Of course, Fr Dominic would have cared little, if at all, of what others thought of him, especially based on his appearance. Once more he made his way to Oscott. He had assumed that his stay there was to be but very brief—instead it was to last four months as questions over the move to Aston were still not settled. In a letter to his cousin, Mrs Canning, written months earlier, Spencer outlined the cause of the problem:

> The difficulty now in the way, is that the Priest who now holds the Mission of Aston Hall, has established himself there at considerable expense, and is not likely to be very easily removable, unless some good arrangement can be devised for him; and of course it is not wished to discompose anyone, who has done nothing to deserve it. If it was not for this, I fancy Padre Domenico might come to the place next week; and I do hope that the prayers which have brought him so far, will not lose their force, but bring him further, even to his end, and that before summer is out, we shall see them settled here.[143]

That was, as Spencer ever was, optimistic. Fr Dominic was once again left waiting: unable to preach or to engage with the English he grew restless but, perhaps thinking of all the obstacles that had been overcome before he had been able to arrive in England, he decided to stay. 'I trust more in the prayers of distant friends, he wrote to the General five days after landing in England, 'than in the activities of those near at hand ... The devil does everything possible to frustrate us. More than once I almost decided to leave and return to Belgium, and I would have done so, had I not looked beyond the housetops.'[144]

He remained at Oscott and Wisemann and Spencer accommodated him as best as they could, as Spencer wrote in another letter to his cousin:

> Padre Domenico has had his cross to bear with
> us, all this time; it is not like what usually makes
> crosses for people. He mourns over having
> plenty to eat, having windows which keep the
> weather out, having chairs to sit *on*, and tables
> to sit *at*, and longs to be in his house, which I
> suppose will not have much of all this trouble
> to him. I have tried to console him now and
> then, which I do by telling him that I never hear
> of anything brought about in our ecclesiastical
> arrangements without long delay, and yet all
> comes right at last, with patience. I tell him
> also that he must have known enough of the
> deliberativeness with which things of the kind
> are settled by the known slowness of all things
> at Rome.[145]

As Fr Dominic's English improved, he was able to
give spiritual conferences to the seminarians and
may have also given lectures in philosophy and theology. He also used his time to work on another work
of apologetics, *A Pacific Discussion*,[146] and study and
practice his English. He went about Oscott in his
Passionist habit and lived according to Passionist
customs as much as possible rising every night with
Spencer to chant Matins and Lauds, praying at other
times during day and night for hours upon end.

Gradually Fr Dominic's eyes were opened to the
reality of the state of the Catholic Church in England.
He could see the timidity of some who were afraid
of upsetting the status-quo and perhaps losing new-
found freedoms. He could sense that the Church was
lacking in the zeal he believed she should have. But,

and perhaps worst of all, he became aware of a lack of unity and charity among Catholics themselves, writing:

> It is true that there is little unity among the Protestants, but there is also little among the Catholics, and this is a great evil ... Oh! If only the Catholics were all that they ought to be!!! But there is too much egoism; too much politics and too little charity ... Everything is calculated, but calculations serve to make good mathematicians, but not good Christians.[147]

As a newcomer to the Church in England it is not surprising that Fr Dominic could misjudge the situation into which he was being immersed. He particularly overestimated the influence of the Tractarian movement on the country and thus how prepared England was to be reconciled with the Catholic Church. Yet even here the seeds of his influence were undoubtedly sewn as he met four leading Tractarians—Ward, Oakley, Smith and Bloxam—at Oscott.

The months rolled on and still, with the new year of 1842, there was no sign that the priest in charge of Aston, Fr Hulme, was willing to relinquish his position, in fact his parishioners had organised a petition to try to ensure that he stayed. Having expressed his sadness to the General, the General wrote back to Fr Dominic encouraging him to stay, at least until he was certain that he was not wanted in Britain. Then, quite suddenly, on the evening of 16 February Fr Hulme arrived at Oscott to bring Fr Dominic and his companion to Aston. The next day Fr Dominic wrote to the General to let him know the 'consoling news' that finally he had 'the long-deferred happiness of seeing our first House in England'.[148]

✢ 19 ✢

Aston

Fr Dominic was delighted with his new abode—
as Wiseman had promised it was ideal to serve
as a Passionist retreat. On the very day of his
arrival he, his brother priest and two aspirants began
the full night and day observance of the customary
rhythm of Passionist prayers.

The parishioners of Aston, however, did not welcome the new arrivals and were openly hostile to
them in and without the church, openly laughing
at their poor grasp of English pronunciation. On 26
April Fr Dominic wrote to the General:

> This foundation was made on the feast of the
> Lance and Nails, and nails there will always
> be. Up to now they have never been wanting—
> and long hard ones at that! At times they seem
> unbearable. To report them all in detail would
> take too long. God knows them. I only ask you
> to pray for me and the ultimate success of this
> foundation, which was certainly willed by God
> from all eternity, nails included.[149]

For such a sensitive soul as Fr Dominic who loved God
and the people to whom he was sent to serve such

unkindness as the Passionists received was a most bitter trial. After a few weeks Fr Dominic decided to address the parishioners simply and directly:

> I wish to say a few words for your edification, but I cannot do it because I am not yet able to speak English. However I shall say something—a very short sermon! My dear beloved, let you love one another because they who love their brothers accomplish perfectly the will of God. Let you love God, and men for God's sake and you shall be perfectly happy for ever. Amen.[150]

Determined to improve his English, and for the edification of his brethren, Fr Dominic preached a retreat to his confreres which was also attended by his predecessor at Aston, Fr Hulme, who was still very much a presence in the parish, and not the most encouraging presence either. But Fr Hulme was impressed and from then on did encourage Fr Dominic in his ministry, advising him to give a series of talks to the faithful. Encouraged, he gave his first full-length sermon on Passion Sunday. The text of this sermon still exists and is evidence that Fr Dominic had, by and large, mastered the written words of English, if not necessarily their pronunciation. 'He stood up boldly and preached Christ Crucified', recalled one witness, 'but his language was so broken and imperfect that even the pious could not suppress their amusement.'[151] As he began to speak, Fr Dominic apologized to the congregation for the mistakes that they were bound to hear and then, speaking from his heart, said,

I cannot explain to you the feeling of my heart. One thing only I will say to you, that the greatest part of you were not yet born since I was desirous to see you and do something for you ... There are now 28 years since I expect the moment of coming to you. Behold now, by the Providence of God, I come, after many difficulties and troubles. Now I am in the very centre of all my desires upon the earth. Now I have nothing to do but dedicate all my soul, my heart, my entire life, for the glory of God and for your spiritual advantage. I shall begin today, but I hope that I shall not finish till my death.[152]

One account of the time records

He seemed so aflame with zeal that he could not give himself time to learn English, and so he began to preach daily at the 10 o'clock Mass. He said he did it to get practice, and he certainly did practise in patience the poor people who came to hear him, and could not understand half of what he said. His broken English, overlaid with Latin and Italian words, some of them ingeniously anglicised, provided a fascinating mixture for those who could manage to sustain their interest.[153]

The General in Rome seems to have had faith in the nascent community that was struggling to settle at Aston as, on 25 March, two more Passionists arrived, Br Ansanus Romani and Confrater Wulstan Bunn, later Fr Joseph. In early April they were joined by two aspirants and, on 22 July, Fr Gaudentius Rossi, a newly ordained priest, arrived from Rome along with another Confrater who was Scottish and had been recently professed at Ere. While the arrival of all of these was most welcome it also increased Fr Dominic's workload as he had to give lectures in theology and philosophy to the members of his community, all of whom were at different stages of ecclesiastical formation, thus meaning that each lecture was individually tailored to each member of the retreat. Three lectures a day had to be given, all to classes of just one person. 'We do what we can', Fr Dominic wrote to the General, 'and both hands and feet are kept busy, as well as heads.'[154]

Even though he had received seven people into the Catholic Church by June 1842, merely four months after having arrived in Aston, Fr Dominic wrote, 'But how little number, how few! Many promised to me to come for instruction, but I observe a great coldness in them, and I am not able to warm them.'

> I am unable to do anything, my desires are strong but my strengths are weak. My life then is among thorns, and sometimes I am very sorry of my weakness and want of means . . . Oh, if I could find many persons able to labour in the vineyard of God. I can do nothing, nothing, nothing. Italian fire is not enough to enkindle the hearts of English men. For that purpose is necessary the heavenly fire, which comes from God only. Oh my God then, send it upon me and upon all men, especially upon my dear English, upon Catholics, upon Protestants, upon all.[155]

Realizing that there were more Catholics at nearby Stone than at Aston, and in the teeth of opposition by local Catholics, Fr Dominic arranged for a room to be hired at the Crown Inn for the not inconsiderable sum of £12 a year. He did not have the money, but believed that it would come, and so from the first Sunday of Advent, 1842, Mass was once again said in Stone for the first time since the Reformation.

✛ 20 ✛

Stone

L EAVING FR AMEDEUS TO LOOK AFTER ASTON, each
Sunday Fr Dominic and Confrater Augustine
would set out early for Stone, where, until
10am, he would either hear Confessions or assist
Confrater Augustine in giving instruction to Catholics or potential converts. Prayers were publicly
recited from 10am for quarter of an hour before Fr
Dominic would preach until the 11am Mass. Ves-
pers, recited in English, at 3pm were followed by
catechism classes for children and adults.

Sunday at Stone was completed with a lecture
at 6pm for non-Catholics. The success of these surprised everyone—sometimes up to 500 people could
be crowded into the hall with a further 200 outside.
As many turned up early to get a good seat Confrater
Augustine would read to them an account of the life
of St Augustine of Canterbury. With many converts
and a general revival of the spiritual health of the
clergy of the area it is no surprise that opposition
to Fr Dominic's ministry soon reared its head. Fr
Dominic could not but be aware of this, writing to
the General in December 1842:

These ministers are beyond words alarmed, and are doing their utmost to embarrass and hinder me. They preach in their churches at the same hour as I do in order to prevent people from coming to hear me. They have started house to house visiting, with the sole object of exhorting people not to come to me. They have opened a new church close to our own, and placed a new minister in charge! But not one of them has come face to face with me. I hear they are afraid, and have some idea that I am a very learned person. In spite of all their machinations against me, the people, with few exceptions, do not believe them. The concourse of non-Catholics goes on increasing to such good purpose that last Sunday the place was filled to its utmost capacity.[156]

The 'machinations' of those who saw him as an enemy were not limited to just house to house visiting. Youngsters were incited to ambush Fr Dominic as he made his way to Stone. They threw stones and clods of earth at him—only to see him pick up one of the stones and kiss it. One stone gashed his head leaving him marked for life.

As he entered Stone, crowds rushed out to gape at him and insult him, as if he were a savage beast or a public thief. Behind him surged a rabble of all the local wastrels, from whose mouths issued words of ribald and unrepeatable insult. As he passed under the windows, even respectable citizens joined in the outcry and jeered at him as the idolatrous Papist, the stuttering Papist, Padre Demonio, the old devil ... Every doorway and window was full of scoffing spectators.[157]

Having failed to deter Fr Dominic from ministering at Stone other methods were deployed to attempt to disturb his lectures such as unsettling the horses in the stable so that their neighing would distract the hearers of his words, drunken men were sent in the direction of his meetings to sing drunken songs whilst some would plant themselves inside the hall to cough, sneeze, laugh loudly and generally attempt to drown out Fr Dominic's weak voice. Through it all Fr Dominic remained calm and asked those who had come to listen to him to remain likewise and as he would walk back to Aston at the end of the day he would pray the rosary specifically for the intentions of those who had been insulting him, inviting his companion to do likewise. 'He seemed to be', recalled a witness, 'one of the old prophets come back to life again.'[158]

Over time the attacks abated, probably because those planning or taking part in them could see that they made no outward difference but also because the number of those who had warmed to Fr Dominic greatly increased. Fr Dominic felt the strain of it though, writing

> Crosses and afflictions multiply so rapidly and seem so endless that I felt myself at the last extremity and was about to go back to Italy. God has assisted me up to this, and I hope He will continue to do so. How much I have to suffer! Although I have been preparing myself for imaginary trials for 28 years, I find I was not half well enough prepared for the awful reality. The will of God alone keeps me up.[159]

> I spent many years before coming to this island preparing myself at all times for suffering. And now, it seems to me that if I had ever foreseen all that awaited me, I should never have had the courage to step on board ship. Such sufferings, and of every kind, would be too much for a giant. Last Sunday, I broke down and wept bitterly. I can do no more. The cross is too heavy. My God, if You intend to increase it, You must increase my strength too.[160]

These are rare examples of Fr Dominic bearing his soul to a friend, Fr Felix: otherwise his letters throughout this period of his life are sunny and optimistic and by the middle of August 1843, eighty people had been received into the Church.

Opposition to Fr Dominic at Stone, however, had not ceased even if the physical violence had lessened. One Calvinist minister arranged a course of 24 lectures to expose 'Papist errors'. These were timed to begin as Fr Dominic's Sunday lectures concluded. At first attendance at Fr Dominic's lectures tailed off but soon the tables were turned and it was the Calvinist minister who saw his numbers dwindling, not least because those who had attended both sets of talks could not help but compare Fr Dominic favourably due to his kindly style and reasoned content with the black anti-papist exaggerations of the Calvinist. Another minister also tried to derail Fr Dominic's work by initiating house to house visits in order to ply the populace with anti-Catholic tracts. This campaign ended when the minister fled the area with the blacksmith's daughter, having seduced her.

Given that he had said his first Mass in Stone in late November 1842, it is astonishing that on 19 July of the following year the foundation stone of a new church was being laid. A piece of land had been given by Mr James Beech, of Elmhurst House, and the building that was to serve as church and school was designed by Pugin. Seven hundred people trudged through the pouring rain to be present at the ceremony, including the local band, but once the rites of laying of the foundation stone began the rain stopped, only to continue again when the ceremony was finished. The church was opened and blessed nine months later on 22 April 1844.

Just two minutes' walk away from the new church lived a lady who was to be a heroic witness to the love of Christ for the poor: her name was Elizabeth Prout. Attending Benediction in Stone, Elizabeth was suddenly convinced of the presence of Christ in the Eucharist and sought reception into the Catholic Church. Deeply attracted by the spirituality of St Paul of the Cross and impressed by the missionary work of the Passionists, she was to go on to found the Sisters of the Cross and Passion.

With a new church, and an increasingly supportive town, Fr Dominic felt emboldened to hold an outside Corpus Christi procession that same year, the first such procession in England since the Reformation. Colourful elements of Italian village life were recreated in the streets of Stone, as Fr Dominic excitedly wrote to the General:

Last Thursday the Feast of Corpus Christi, we had a beautiful procession in our grounds, with all possible splendour—triumphal arches, altars, and a sermon preached out of doors. There were present fully a thousand people, half of whom were Protestants. Yesterday we repeated the ceremony, and it was even more magnificent. I believe there were over a thousand Protestants there, and as many Catholics from all parts. I hope that it will not go without fruit. Such things have never been seen in these countries. You should scarcely believe the impression that is made on our own Catholic people, and the enthusiasm excited, as well as the wonderment of the Protestants, astounded at their first sight of the magnificence of Catholic worship.[161]

The procession the following year was even more successful in terms of attendance with newspaper adverts in local papers helping to attract over five thousand souls to the proceedings.

Meanwhile back at Aston, Fr Dominic remained busy. By 1843 he was giving three lectures a day to his community as well as fulfilling the demands of the liturgy, giving lectures, preaching and general housework. One sermon on Church unity was so highly thought of by those who heard it that it was published in September 1843. 'In his sermons', a witness remembered, 'he spoke familiarly, simply, almost like a child ... His sermons always made a lasting impression on all of us.'[162] Frequent themes were the Passion, the Sacraments and the rosary.

As well as doing his own work, Fr Dominic also assisted others: for Fr Gaudentius he wrote a series of short meditations, for Fr Joseph, then preaching at the new church at Stone, Fr Dominic provided sermons and to a priest at Ere he sent thirty sets of sermon notes. Despite all this Fr Dominic was always 'most exact and faithful in the observance of the Rule' rarely missing a community obligation. 'His humility', recorded Br Seraphim, 'made him believe, in practice, that he was not the superior. He carried abnegation to the point of ignoring himself altogether.'[163]

For other members of his community, however, whilst expecting the Rule to be followed, he was watchful for any whom he felt might have been unnecessarily austere on themselves. When the abstemiousness of two of the younger brothers was brought to Fr Dominic's attention, he would say to them, 'I will pay the butcher and the baker, but not the doctor'.[164]

His community recalled how, if Fr Dominic had been away, he used to address them on his return with the simple and sincere words 'My dear children, I have been away from you, but you have been in my heart all the time'. He would follow this with a brief account of his time away often concluding with the words, 'Love God, my dear children, love God'.[165]

21

Missions and Retreats

B ETWEEN 24 AND 31 MARCH 1844, Fr Dominic
gave his first mission in England at Lane End,
Staffordshire. This was the first mission to
given in England in centuries for Fr Dominic and the
Rosminian, Fr Gentili, reintroduced this source and
method of growth that was to flourish in the British
Isles over the next hundred years.

Given the importance of the occasion for Fr Dominic in terms of his hopes for his mission in England
as a whole, it can be imagined that he was more
sensitive than ever to whether or not the people who
came would understand him. The result of his nerves
was that his English was worse than usual and was,
as far as he could judge from the facial reactions of
his listeners, simply an embarrassment. Throughout the following day his nerves about the evening
sermon only increased and he anxiously wondered
would anyone come after his performance the previous evening. They did come, but a full night and day
of worry did not equip him to speak any more clearly
than the night before. As soon as he finished speaking, he fled to the safety of the sacristy distressed at

having let down the priest who had invited him, the congregation and himself. But he was immediately followed into the sacristy by a well-built Irishman who knelt at his feet begging him to hear his Confession. Upon inquiring which part of his sermon had so moved the man to such prompt repentance, the Irishman responded,

> Your reverence, the whole sermon struck me all of a heap; I did not understand more than a few words of it, and don't know from Adam what foreign language you were talking. But I saw you stretch out your arms, and your voice had something so kind in it, that I said to myself, though I am the biggest blackguard in the whole Church—more shame on me!—that holy man won't scold me, and I'll make my confession to him.[166]

The chap was heaven sent and, with greater confidence, Fr Dominic continued giving the mission which ultimately he judged to have succeeded beyond his expectations.

Many more missions followed, Fr Dominic receiving such a multitude of invitations that, to his great regret, he was unable to accept them all. Writing to the General, Fr Gaudentius reported that 'After almost two years of obscurity … this torch, so bright and scorching, begins to diffuse the light of doctrine and divine fire'.

> The name of Fr Dominic becomes every day more famous. With good reason he is considered by almost all the Catholics and by many of those Protestants who have made his acquaintance

as a man altogether extraordinary. One man
at Swynnerton said: 'Fr Dominic is a saint on
earth.' One parish priest called him a 'second
St Ligouri' ... Wherever he goes, Fr Dominic
works wonders. The churches are often too
small for the crowds ... In recreation his English
is poor, but when he preaches, it is correct; in
fact, the dean of one district said that he spoke
exceedingly well. His style, so plain, homely,
affectionate and chatty, and his simple and
humble ways, surprise everybody and steal the
hearts of his audience, who are used to hearing
a more formal and stilted sort of sermon.[167]

Despite poor health, Fr Dominic travelled the length
of the country to give missions and retreats: from
York, Manchester and Liverpool, to Birmingham,
Stafford and Wolverhampton and to London, Ware
and Winchester to name but a few he went to preach.
His Confessional was besieged and he was often kept
in it until the early hours of the morning due to the
throng of people who came to him. He knew himself,
from frequent personal experience, the importance
of being a penitent. As such he wanted to reveal his
life to his confessor so that the confessor was able
'to read the most secret and intimate sentiments of
his heart, his hiding places, agitations, temptations
and depressions'.[168] And so, as a young priest, he
resolved that

In hearing confessions and directing souls,
before I say anything at all, I will always raise
my mind to heaven and ask Our Lady to obtain
for me the necessary lights to direct them
well. My dear Mamma, from now on, I wish

to consecrate to you all those souls who will
ever put themselves under my direction, and
especially those who have done so already. I
wish to employ all your graces to adorn your
crown. I will strive to form them exteriorly; you
must look after them interiorly.[169]

Fr Dominic's reputation went before him and the
faithful flocked to his missions, some walking over
thirty miles to do so, though they knew that they
would not understand all, or perhaps even most,
of what he said: they sensed that here was a genu-
inely holy man. An account of one of his missions
undoubtedly stands for the experience of many:

In his instructions he displays a shrewd and
ready wit, a fine imagination and a penetrating
and solid judgment. Above all, there is an aura
of piety and charity that charms and persuades
his hearers to be convinced by his forcible
arguments. A proof of this is their eager and
patient attendance in spite of difficulties and
disadvantages. For, though his language is
good, his pronunciation is defective, so that
it is hard to understand him, and his manner
and delivery must appear strange to an English
audience. Yet the country people rose early,
walked far, waited long in the cold and bad
weather, and many conversions were the result.
He had assistants in the confessional, but all
wanted the preacher, and indeed, he laboured
very hard.[170]

As well as having a profound effect on the laity Fr
Dominic also had many opportunities to influence
the clergy through retreats that he gave at Oscott,

Bishop Eton, St Edmund's Ware, Prior Park, York, Ushaw College and to Fr Faber's community at Cotton, at the very least fifteen retreats in all. Of those he was addressing he wrote, 'The English clergy ... are good, and I have always loved and respected them. I think that many of them are fond of me too, because I have never reprimanded them, but have always treated them with the greatest respect.'[171]

Unfortunately, none of the texts of these retreats have survived but it is known that they all centred on the Passion and the love of God and were intended to encourage his listeners, never to reprimand them. Some flavour of his approach can be garnered from words he spoke to his own young Passionist priests: 'Use mildness with the English', he advised them, 'and you will attain everything; use harshness, and you will attain nothing, absolutely nothing.'[172] His was the gentleness of St Francis de Sales:

> I believe that even the incredulous would re-enter on the way of salvation, if we invited them to touch our hearts, i.e., if we treated them with kindness and urbanity. I can speak from experience. Once, when I had failed to convince an unbeliever with arguments, I finally said to him: 'My dear brother, what more can I do for you? Ah, if only I could give my life and my blood for you, how happy I should be!' At once this unbeliever flung himself at my feet, and seizing me by the knees, burst into a flood of tears, and exclaimed 'Father, father, you have won'.[173]

The very manner in which he gave his retreats

invited the openness of the priests taking part. He would always appoint someone to prompt him if he could not find the right word to say. This left room for humour if the prompter so wished, humour that Fr Dominic warmly welcomed as he laughed at himself with those in front of him. On the last evening of the retreat Fr Dominic always asked permission for the priests to be allowed to talk, preferring to avoid illicit breaches of the rule of silence but surely also understanding how little time the priests at the retreat were to spend together and hoping that any conversation would be fruitfully guided by what they had heard and experienced.

Convents also enjoyed the fruits of Fr Dominic's retreats. The Sisters of Mercy and the Benedictine nuns were the first to get to know him and eagerly shared with their sisters in other houses the news of his sanctity. Thus Fr Dominic came to preach in nearly all the convents of these orders in England. Of the Sisters of Mercy in Birmingham he wrote, 'They ought to be regarded as Apostles rather than Nuns. The good they do is immense. The Anglicans are more afraid of them than of the missioners.'[174] Bishop Walsh was particularly keen that the convents of the Midlands should know Fr Dominic and the bishop appointed him 'extraordinary' confessor of the Benedictine Convent of Heywood (this later moved to Colwich) of which Fr Dominic exclaimed that it was one of the finest convents that he had ever seen. That the convent had been founded expressly to pray for the conversion of England filled Fr Dominic's heart with the greatest joy. Of Fr Dominic the Prioress, Mother M. Clare, wrote,

> From the first moment that I met Fr Dominic, I esteemed him as a man full of the spirit of God, animated by great zeal for God's glory, poor in spirit and in fact, and perfectly detached from everything human, who lived on earth as a stranger and pilgrim, and whose only consolation was in heaven and in discussing God and heavenly things. His profound knowledge and great natural talents were hidden under a veil of the most profound humility. His whole deportment, and all his words and actions on each and every occasion adumbrated perfect sweetness, self-abnegation and humility of heart. All these qualities, united to a rare simplicity, were mirrored on his face, which it was impossible to look at without being convinced of his authentic sanctity. We could never induce him to prolong his visits beyond the time necessary for the fulfilment of his spiritual duties, and he left without delay as soon as they were finished; yet, such was his graciousness that if a lay-sister or the youngest novice asked for advice, he gave it with as much charity and patience as to the superior herself. I cannot find words adequate to express my esteem for this great Servant of God.[175]

22

Littlemore

A DECADE BEFORE COMING TO ENGLAND, writing to a fellow Passionist, Fr Dominic considered how one might go about convincing non-Catholics to approach and enter into life in the Catholic Church:

> We should never irritate inquirers, but strive to win them over to the Truth gently, appealing to the heart rather than the ear. We must never use cutting expressions, but excel in kindness in our approach, as the best apologists have always done, e.g. Bossuet, from whose writings I have learned much.
>
> To become a Catholic must not be made to seem difficult; the path to the Church must be smoothed as much as possible. For example, in many questions, we could show that agreement could be reached simply by clearly stating our respective points of view, which are not really opposed. This was Bossuet's method with a Protestant Abbe.
>
> We should be on our guard not to 'canonize' all the conduct of Catholics. We should not hesitate to admit that, amongst us, there have been — and still are — disorders of various kinds which we would gladly see eliminated. In this

way we do not leave ourselves open to attack on the basis of abuses already admitted. In dogmatic questions, however, we must make it quite clear that there is not, and cannot be, any real ground for attack or cavilling.

It would be well to emphasise that salvation is possible for Protestants in good faith, if they act according to their lights.[176]

Fr Dominic had been aware of the Tractarian movement long before he came to England. In spring 1841, while he was still living in Belgium, he was sent a copy of an article published by John Dobree Dalgairns (1818–76) that explained the Tractarians' position. The article was not actually credited to Dalgairns but simply to 'a young member of the University'. Fr Dominic, who thought that the writer was representing the whole professorial staff of the University of Oxford, considered publishing a response but, after long prayer, decided instead to send his response to the author of the article. He then realized that as he did not know who the author was, he did not know where to send his response. But he felt sure that someone as well connected as Fr Spencer would be able to detect who the author was, so, in the late summer of 1841, to Spencer he sent his manuscript. Spencer forwarded it on to Bloxam, Newman's curate at Littlemore, who in turn passed it on to Dalgairns. 'You cannot imagine', Dalgairns was to write later, 'how greatly I have longed after you in Christ ever since I received your letters.' Both he and Bloxam had been profoundly moved by Dominic's writing to them and it is beyond question that these two men proceeded to discuss Fr Dominic's letter with Newman as well as other fellow Tractarians.

Dalgairns's letter had been published in *L'Univers* and sought the sympathy of Catholics for the Church of England as, he claimed, the Thirty-Nine Articles could not be considered in opposition to Catholic beliefs. He enumerated, in conciliatory fashion, issues that both Catholics and Anglicans would need to address before full reconciliation was possible. 'Let there be found amongst them a saint like the Seraph of Assisi', he wrote, 'and the union of the Churches will be effected.'

What seemed to particularly impress Dalgairns and his associates in Fr Dominic's response was his affectionate and irenic tone that demonstrated a desire for dialogue with them that was undoubtedly every bit as strong as their wish to converse with the Roman Church. No other response had been anything like this: they were even treated with a reverence that was normally reserved only for Catholic clergy themselves: 'I write to you as friends and brothers', wrote Fr Dominic, addressing his interlocutors as 'beloved brethren'. Having showed Dalgairns the greatest warmth and courtesy, Fr Dominic then proceeds to clearly and politely disagree with the tenets of Dalgairns's published letter, not least in asking how various of the Thirty-Nine Articles could 'be reconciled with the faith of the Catholic Church and the Tridentine Decrees' to which, wrote Fr Dominic, they were either 'diametrically opposed' or at least 'sufficiently out of accord'. The central issue, however, was that of authority: how could more than one Church claim to exercise the divinely instituted gift of authority?

> Christ did not found two or three Churches, but only one, as faith teaches; you yourselves confess one only Church and chant with us the Nicene Creed. If, notwithstanding her supposed practical errors, the Roman Church is true and Catholic, it follows that all Churches which differ from her are not true, and salvation cannot be had in them, unless good faith or invincible ignorance plead excuse. Except in cases of invincible ignorance or good faith, all who are formally out of the Church are not in the way of salvation. Therefore everyone is bound to enter the true Church, and remain in it if he wishes to be saved.[177]

Given the logical clarity of the reasons why the Oxford men should become Catholics, Fr Dominic suggested that it was 'reverence for your fathers' that detained them and 'the hope of bringing them over with you'. This reasoning, he proposed, was 'more of the flesh than of the spirit. Christ more than once rebuked this kind of delay. Who knows but that, while you are waiting, death may come and you may have to hear "I called you and you refused".' Fr Dominic knew from the *L'Univers* article that the Tractarians argued that 'it is better to bring all in than some'. He disagreed, writing with incontrovertible Gospel simplicity, 'Is it not better to bring in some than none? Must we leave good alone to wait for better? It is a tedious process, you say, to bring a whole nation to the faith one by one, but was not this the way in which the nations were converted?' Fr Dominic was always polite, immensely respectful and warm, and simply expressed the belief of the Church that the Church of England was not a branch of the Catholic Church.[178]

Fr Dominic's letter had been written in Latin, thus Dalgairns chose to respond in Latin himself. He gently disagreed with Fr Dominic writing that apostolic succession, sanctity, orthodoxy and persecution were clear marks of the Church of England that was, he wrote, indeed part of the Catholic Church, albeit a sick part of it. He also wrote that 'a fire of love was kindled in the hearts of all those who read your words so pregnant with love. Like burning arrows, your words went straight to the heart of all those who read them.'[179] From a letter of Fr Dominic to the General we know that Dalgairns had said of Fr Dominic's letter that he had 'read it on his knees and his reading was interrupted by tears'.[180]

Fr Dominic and Dalgairns exchanged further correspondence, all written with great courtesy, Fr Dominic continuing to address his interlocuters as 'My dear brethren in Christ' and asking their forgiveness 'for not having always had as good an opinion of you as I have now'.[181]

After the controversy that Newman and his followers were exposed to following the publication of Tract 90, wherein Newman argued that the Thirty-Nine articles could be held to along with Catholic doctrine, he asked that his closest associates should refrain from further contact with Catholics, for fear that if the news of such correspondence were to reach the press his already precarious position would become utterly untenable. Fr Dominic was the sole Catholic whom Newman permitted members of his community to maintain contact with. But even after Fr Dominic came to England, it was not deemed wise that he and any of the fellowship at Littlemore should meet. 'It is one of the most painful of the many painful things which beset us in our present position', wrote Dalgairns to Fr Dominic on 31 October 1842, 'that we cannot hold intercourse with men whom we hold so dear as I do you, if you will permit me to say so.' 'We', note. Fr Dominic did not simply happen to turn up at Littlemore on the night of 8 October 1845 to receive Newman into the Church as if he were almost a stranger—they, through Dalgairns, had been in contact through over four years of correspondence previously.

At Dalgairns's request, Fr Dominic sent him a copy of the Passionist Rule, including a copy of *The Lament of England* in the package. Of the Rule Dalgairns commented, 'it was read by me and others here with much interest; it seems a very happy combination of the contemplative and active life'. Dalgairns and his companions were also most grateful for the copy of *The Lament*:

> I thank you very much for having sent me your pamphlet; I am sure we English ought to feel most grateful to God for having inspired you with such sentiments towards us. It cannot be

that these feelings should be suffered to fall to the ground fruitless, for they are God's work. He would not have once kindled such a flame of love in the heart of Christendom if He did not intend to bring something out of it. Not only has your heart warmed towards us, but our hearts have also been set on fire by the same flame. I do hope that all this points to the reunion of England with the Catholic Church, but when or how we cannot tell . . . Whenever you have a moment to spare, it will give me great pleasure to have a line from you.[182]

It is certain that Newman shared Dalgairns's appreciation of Fr Dominic,[183] and a respect that took the risk of attracting negative notice by inviting Fr Dominic to Littlemore in June 1844. It was to be a visit of critical importance to Newman and the Littlemore community, not due to anything in particular that was said but rather due to whom they perceived Fr Dominic to be. Newman could not see how the Church of England could not be a branch of the Catholic Church when ringing notes of sanctity were to be found within it. And where, he asked and not in a rhetorical fashion, was such evidence in the Church of Rome? As Newman wrote to Bloxham,

That we must change too I do not deny. Rome must change *first of all in her spirit*. We must see more sanctity in her than we do at present. Alas! I see no marks of sanctity, or if any, they are chiefly confined to converts from us. 'By their fruits you shall know them' is the main canon Our Lord gives us to know true Pastors from false. I do verily think that, with all our sins, there is more sanctity in the Church of England

and Ireland than in the Roman Catholic bodies in the same countries. I say not this in reproach, but in great sorrow. Indeed, I am ever making the best of things before others when Roman Catholics are attacked; but I cannot deny this great lack. What Hildebrand did by faith and holiness they do by political intrigue. They join with those who are further from them in Creed to oppose those who are nearer to them. Never can I think such ways the footsteps of Christ. If they want to convert England, let them go barefooted into our manufacturing towns — let them preach to the people like St Francis Xavier — let them be pelted and trampled on, and I will own that they do what we cannot. I will confess they are our betters far. I will (though I could not on that account join them) I would gladly incur their reproach. This is to be Catholics, this is to secure a triumph. Let them use the proper arms of the Church and they will prove that they are the Church by using them — what a day it will be if God ever raises up holy men, Bernards or Borromeos, in their communion! But even if this were done, difficulties would not be at an end, though I think, sanctity being secured, everything would ultimately follow.[184]

These were words that Dalgairns had echoed in his article in *L'Univers* where he wrote,

> Let them go into our great cities to preach the Gospel to this half-pagan people, let them walk barefoot; let them clothe themselves in sackcloth; let the spirit of mortification be apparent in their looks; in a word, let there be found among them a saint in the measure of the Seraph of Assisi, and the heart of England is already won.[185]

As Pope St Paul VI was to say at Fr Dominic's beatification in 1963, 'We must grant a further merit to our new Beatus, it is that of having carried in himself the image most likely to win the esteem and admiration of Newman'. 'I have been interested in your account of your labours in Staffordshire', wrote Dalgairns to Fr Dominic; 'You are, I am sure, taking the right way to win the English heart.'

> The English Catholics seem to fancy that they can do a great deal by copes and chasubles and beautiful music; they are, however, mistaken; let them try to cope with those evils which our system has all but given up in despair; let them preach barefoot in the streets of our great towns, and depend upon it, they will force England, or at least all who are worth having in England, to look upon them in a very different light from what they do now.[186]

Dalgairns rightly credits Fr Dominic for the mission that he was accomplishing whilst not realising, yet, that there were many others who had faithfully and at great personal cost to themselves trudged their way along lane and street from the time of rack and dungeon through the time of hidden growth until the time when such growth could visibly begin to flourish. No wonder, given what was passing, that many Catholics of the early nineteenth century rejoiced in the outward signs of the mysteries that were so loved and cherished. And, on the whole, they did this while also relieving the lives of the poorest, their flocks, as best as they could.

Yet Fr Dominic was indubitably the very man that the community of Littlemore needed God to send them as Newman was to write, many years later, 'When his form came in sight, I was moved to the depths in the strangest way. His very look had about it something holy.' His heart was won.

Fr Dominic's impression of Newman and his disciples was of being received 'with every token of cordiality and sincere regard ... These men work like martyrs for a good cause.'[187] Correspondence with Dalgairns continued, Fr Dominic being consulted on various matters. They knew that they could trust him asking, on one occasion, for a supply of hair-shirts. 'Could you put us in the way of getting a dozen such implements?' wrote Dalgairns in October 1844,

> They will be put into the hands of a person who guides many souls among us, so you need not fear their being indiscreetly used ... The person who wishes for them would mind no expense in procuring them and would be glad to pay for them. I had almost forgotten to say that he also wants a discipline, such as ordinary persons would use. Of course, he wishes his request to be a secret.[188]

The 'person who guides many souls' was clearly Newman and Newman clearly knew of the asceticism of Fr Dominic. In fact, he knew of this so well that he was careful to ask for a discipline 'such as ordinary persons would use', Newman rightly suspecting that his saintly Passionist used a more rigorous discipline than others might: Fr Dominic's discipline consisted of steel blades.

The following month Dalgairns wrote once more to Fr Dominic declaring

> You cannot tell what a comfort your charitable sympathy is to me. Pray for me, pray for us all, and especially for Mr Newman who is always glad to hear news about yourself. As I am more open with you than I should be with almost anyone else, I beg of you not to show my letters to anyone.[189]

Dalgairns continued to seek Fr Dominic's prayers and finally, on 20 September 1845, he wrote asking that Fr Dominic receive him into the Catholic Church and for this to take place at Aston as 'I can think of no better place than your house. The uniformly kind expressions which you have ever used towards me make me feel sure that I shall be welcome.'[190] One can only guess the prayers and mortifications that Fr Dominic had offered up for Newman and his disciples during these years and the joy with which he greeted Dalgairns's news. He was ecstatic and responded to Dalgairns with alacrity: 'Benedictus Deus qui non amovit orationem meam et misericordiam suam a me' [Blessed be God, who hath not turned away my prayer, nor his mercy from me]. It will be more easy for you to imagine than for me to describe the pleasure which your kind letter gave me. What happiness, what joy to my heart!' Fr Dominic was happy to openly express that he prayed and believed that Dalgairns's conversion was but the opening of a new season of grace in the British Isles, concluding his letter with a remembrance of Dalgairns's illustrious companions, in words of typical Barberi graciousness: 'Will you be so kind as to present my best respects to the Rev. Mr Newman, Mr St John, and all your holy companions of Littlemore'. Fr Dominic's heart was full as he wrote

> Dear Littlemore, I love thee! A little more and we shall see happy results from Littlemore. When the learned and holy Superior of Littlemore will come, then I hope we shall see the beginning of a new era. Yes, we shall see again the happy days of Augustine, of Lanfranc, and of Thomas. England will be once more the Isle of Saints, and nurse of New Christian nations, destined to carry the light of the Gospels *coram gentibus et regibus et filiis Israel* [to the gentiles and their kings and the sons of Israel].[191]

Dalgairns made his profession of faith 'with extraordinary fervour' before Fr Dominic at Aston on the 29 September, 1845, the feast of St Michael the Archangel.[192] On returning to Littlemore Newman observed 'how happy and altered' Dalgairns was: 'you would wonder', Newman wrote to a friend, 'I cannot describe it, but it is the manner of a person entrusted with a great gift'.[193]

23

Newman

B EFORE DALGAIRNS LEFT ASTON, Fr Dominic
inquired as to whether he thought that Newman might also soon become a Catholic. Dalgairns knew that Fr Dominic was the ideal priest to
encourage Newman to make the decisive step and
so, with Newman's permission, it was arranged that
Fr Dominic would call in at Littlemore as he made
his way to Belgium where he was due to carry out
the annual visitation. Yet having returned to Littlemore, Dalgairns thought it prudent to warn Fr Dominic against expecting too much to happen too soon:

> I write a line to say that I hope you will come
> here as you intended. I cannot say that I see
> any immediate good likely to come from your
> visit; but it will be a great good to give me the
> pleasure of seeing you as well as Mr Newman
> and our whole community ... When I say that
> I see no prospect of any immediate good from
> your coming, I do not mean to say that no good
> whatsoever can result. It will be a great good
> to keep up intercourse between Littlemore and
> Aston Hall.[194]

The very next day Dalgairns wrote again to Fr Dominic:

When I wrote to you I was not aware of a circumstance, which makes it very likely that there should be some work for you to do. I think I had better not tell you what it is lest I should disappoint you, as it may not take place after all. But I think I am right in begging you to come on the chance of it. I say no more just now as I hope to have the pleasure of seeing you soon.[195]

A fragment of a letter from Dalgairns that is held in the Archives of Brompton Oratory reveals the reason for Dalgairns renewed hope:

The Superior of the house (i.e. Fr Dominic) asked my leave to come and see Newman on his way to Belgium. Newman surprised me when I mentioned this to him by saying that he would be received then. He felt, as I did, that he was only keeping all his friends in suspense; and there were certain things connected with the order of Passionists which made him think it almost providential that Fr Dominic came at that time to Littlemore. The Order had always prayed, especially for England, and the founder of it had once seen a vision during Mass of his Monks preaching in England.[196]

Yet Newman remained uncertain if the time had really come for him to be received into the Church by Fr Dominic, writing on 4 October that it was 'likely' that he would be received during Fr Dominic's visit but he was not sure.[197] Ultimately Newman was looking for a providential sign that he should become a Catholic so that the decision would be made not trusting in the strength of his own intellectual inquiry or his feelings alone. In Fr Dominic, with the history of St Paul of the Cross before him—a history of which, very unusually, Newman was aware—Newman perceived the hand of God. As he wrote to a friend, Henry Wilberforce, on 7 October, 'Having all along gone so simply and entirely by my own reason, I was not sorry ... to submit myself to what seemed an external call'.[198] On the same day he wrote to another friend saying 'And since I had all along been forced to act by my own judgement, I was not sorry for what seemed an external call to which I should show obedience'.[199] This admission was repeated by Newman in a letter of the following day:

> And since I had all along been obliged to act from my own sense of right, I was not sorry that an external call, as it might seem, should come and cut short my time, and remind me of the sudden summons of St Matthew or St Peter, and of the awful suddenness of the judgement.[200]

Again and again Newman's letters reveal that the fact that Fr Dominic had been sent to England 'without any act of his own', as Newman saw it, deeply impressed him. The story of the Passionists, especially regarding St Paul of the Cross, also left an indelible impression, the founder, the order and Fr Dominic (in the recognizable guise of Fr Domenico de Matre Dei) all making a substantial appearance in Newman's novel, *Loss and Gain*, that was written just two years after his conversion. In numerous letters Newman demonstrates that he had closely observed

Fr Dominic both in person and, through what he had heard of him, from afar. He wrote to Wilberforce, 'He is a simple quaint man, an Italian; but a very sharp clever man too in his way';[201] to Mrs Bowden, 'He is a shrewd clever man, but as unaffected and simple as a child; and most singularly kind in his thoughts of religious persons in our communion. I wish all persons were as charitable as I know him to be. I believe him to be a very holy man';[202] to R. W. Church, 'He is a simple, holy man, and withal gifted with remarkable powers';[203] and to Isaac Williams, 'He is full of love for religious men among us, and believes many to be inwardly knit to the Catholic Church who are outwardly separate from it'.[204] Alfred Wilson sums up Fr Dominic's critical importance to Newman by writing,

> From all this it is clear that Fr Dominic's part in Newman's conversion was neither incidental nor accidental. The widespread idea that he was merely the lucky one who happened to turn up at the right moment, is totally false. He did not simply profit by the occasion; his personality and holiness made the occasion.[205]

In 1875 Cardinal Newman was happy to contribute these words to the process for Fr Dominic's beatification:

> He had a great part in my own conversion and in that of others. When his form came into sight, I was moved to the depths in the strangest way. His very look had about it something holy. The gaiety and affability of his manner in the midst

of all his sanctity was in itself a holy sermon.
No wonder that I became his convert and his
penitent. He was a great lover of England. His
sudden death filled me with grief. I hoped and
still hope that Rome will crown him with the
aureole of the saints.[206]

And so, on Wednesday 8 October Dalgairns and St
John set out to meet Fr Dominic, Dalgairns giving
this account of how events then unfolded:

At that time all of us except St. John, though
we did not doubt Newman would become
a Catholic, were anxious and ignorant of his
intentions in detail. About 3 o'clock I went to
take my hat and stick and walk across the fields
to the Oxford 'Angel' where the coach stopped.
As I was taking my stick Newman said to me
in a very low and quiet tone: 'When you see
your friend, will you tell him that I wish him
to receive me into the Church of Christ?' I said:
'Yes' and no more. I told Fr. Dominic as he was
dismounting from the top of the coach. He said:
'God be praised,' and neither of us spoke again
till we reached Littlemore.[207]

To reach Oxford, Fr Dominic had booked an outside
seat of a stagecoach, leaving Aston at 10am and arriving in Oxford twelve hours later. Most of the journey
had been in torrential rain and he was soaked to the
skin. He probably had not eaten on the journey and,
even when he arrived at Littlemore an hour before
midnight, he still declined food. As he began to dry
his sodden clothes in front of a blazing fire in the
hearth the door to the room opened, Fr Dominic
stood and Newman cast himself on his knees in front

of him seeking admission into the Catholic Church. 'Outside', wrote Oakley, 'the rain came down in torrents and the wind, like a spent giant, howled from the expiring notes of its equinoctial fury': a dying storm without, and within the heart of John Henry Newman who began his confession, completing it the following morning. The feelings within Newman's heart were almost certainly those he ascribed to Charles Reding in *Loss and Gain* when Reding presents himself, as Newman did, to the Passionist priest seeking to be received into the Church:

> Charles's feelings were indescribable, but all pleasurable. His heart beat, not with fear or anxiety, but from the thrill of delight ... His trouble went in a moment, and he could have laughed for joy. He could hardly keep his countenance, and almost feared to be taken for a fool ... The good Father smiled ... Charles and he soon came to an understanding.[208]

Fr Dominic also left an account of the scene that unfolded at Littlemore on that stormy October night:

> What a spectacle it was for me, to see at my feet John Henry Newman begging me to hear his confession and admit him into the bosom of the Catholic Church. There by the fire he began his general confession with extraordinary humility and devotion. Next day at six o'clock in the evening, Richard Stanton, Frederick Bowles and Newman made their profession of faith with such fervour and piety that I was almost beside myself with joy.[209]

The morning after, Fr Dominic said Mass at Littlemore, using Henry Wilberforce's desk as an altar, Newman, Stanton and Bowles receiving Holy Communion for the first time alongside Dalgairns and St John. Word of the Newman's reception spread swiftly, a rapturous Wiseman writing to Pope Gregory XVI, who sent Newman his apostolic blessing, commending the zeal of Fr Dominic, who 'spared no pains that he might lead straying sheep to the one fold of Christ'.[210] Fr Dominic's joy was clear for all to see as he organized Masses of thanksgiving in London, Boulogne, Ere and Aston, writing to the General, 'Let us hope that the results of these conversions may be incalculable. All that I have suffered since I left Italy has been well compensated by this happy event.'[211]

The esteem of Newman for Fr Dominic was enduring. Returning from Ere on his way back to Aston, Fr Dominic called again at Littlemore. Dalgairns, who was not present at this time but heard of it from the community, wrote to Fr Dominic saying, 'I heard from Mr St John about your visit to Littlemore and how glad they all were to see you ... I hope that you will continue to see much of Mr Newman. Pray, tell him openly and without fear what you think. He will be glad to know your thoughts on all points.'[212] Indeed, Newman and Fr Dominic exchanged six letters between 14 and 23 December 1845 as Newman decided what to do next. Fr Dominic was moved by Newman's docility as a new Catholic and Newman continued to be impressed by Fr Dominic's disinterested encouragement, writing some years later, 'If there be those who would not try to make you theirs, it is the Passionists. Dear Fr Dominic never made any advances—he was most delicate—though his want of novices was his most keen and continual trial.'[213] Ultimately Fr Dominic advised Newman and his companions to become Oratorians, Newman writing to Fr Dominic as soon as he himself had come to the same conclusion to let him know the news.

Newman and St. John stayed with Fr Dominic at Aston Hall for two nights over the New Year of 1845/46, Newman taking in his setting and using the Hall as the scene for the reception of Charles Reding into the Church in his novel, *Loss and Gain*. The correspondence between the two holy men continued. Fr Dominic had hoped that Newman would return to Littlemore making it a base to influence the Oxford men, Newman writing to explain to him why this was not possible. Newman also wrote to Fr Dominic explaining why it had become necessary to sell the Littlemore property but before leaving the building for the last time Newman took with him Henry Wilberforce's desk: 'I had not the heart to let it remain behind', he wrote, 'It formed part of the altar at which Fr Dominic offered Mass, and from which I received my first Communion.'[214]

There are frequent references to Fr Dominic in Newman's letters of this time, Newman being particularly happy with Fr Dominic's praise for his newly completed *Development of Doctrine*: 'and, a pre-possessed person, but a shrewd and good and deep divine, Fr Dominic, is pleased with it'.[215] The 'shrewd' Fr Dominic, along with Wiseman, advised Newman to publish this work as an historical document of his Anglican days rather than seek an imprimatur for it. They did not doubt the soundness of the theology in *Development* but could see that at that time it would have garnered a mixed reception from Catholic theologians which would not have been helpful for either Newman or the cause of the conversion of England for which they all longed.

While Newman's conversion was widely reported, and frequently aspects surrounding it were misrepresented, neither Fr Dominic, Newman nor Wiseman wrote publicly about what had actually happened. In response to complaints from some correspondents of the *Tablet*, Fr Dominic decided to write two letters hoping to establish for Newman and his friends the warm welcome into the Catholic Church which he felt that they deserved. He wrote in the most enthusiastic Italian style, resounding with praise for Newman which, of course, acutely embarrassed the converts of Littlemore. 'A Capuchin Monastery', he wrote, 'would appear a palace when compared to Littlemore.' Writing after the letters' publication Newman wrote to a friend, 'Good Fr Dominic has published a second letter to the *Tablet*, which no one here can read with a grave face'.[216] Newman asked Wiseman to gently request that Fr Dominic cease publishing letters about him, Fr Dominic gladly acquiescing in the bishop's decision. Writing to some nuns who asked Fr Dominic why he no longer wrote about Newman's conversion, Fr

Dominic responded, 'The Bishop has forbidden me to write, and WHY is not a question for a subject to ask. Why was the devil's question.'[217]

During his time in Rome Newman made several visits to the Ss John and Paul, pondering on one occasion whether or not St Paul of the Cross should be adopted as the patron saint by the planned English Oratory. The Passionists were always going to hold an esteemed place in Newman's mind as evidenced by his support of their founding a new retreat in Dublin during Newman's sojourn there when he was attempting to found a Catholic university. Later in life when the Oratory had settled in Birmingham, Newman always visited the neighbouring Passionist house at Harborne on the feast of St Paul of the Cross. Newman would refer to Fr Dominic and his sayings in his sermons, implicitly referring to him in his most famous sermon, *The Second Spring*, when, after citing the names of the saints whom would undoubtedly be looking down with delight on the gathering of the First Synod of Westminster said, referring to St George, 'and others also, his equals or his juniors in history whose pictures are above our altars, or soon shall be, the surest proof that the Lord's arm has not waxen short, nor his mercy failed—they, too, are looking down from their thrones on high upon the throng'.[218] A small picture of Fr Dominic hung on the wall of Newman's room, with a Passionist badge given to him by Fr Dominic.

The moment of Newman's conversion was indubitably the happiest event in Fr Dominic's life. The

writer Dom Bede Camm, OSB, asked 'If a conversion is chiefly and necessarily the work of God's
grace in answer to prayer, shall we be wrong if we
attribute to Fr Dominic a far greater share in this
unique conversion than appears or can appear on
the surface?'[219] And as Pope St Paul VI was to say at
Fr Dominic's beatification, 'the drawing together of
these two holy figures, the Blessed Father Dominic
and the Cardinal John Henry Newman, will leave its
mark upon our spirit, that We will continue to think
of the mysterious sense of their meeting with great
hope and with prolonged prayer'.[220]

24

New Foundations

M EANWHILE AT ASTON, despite the comings and goings of many novices, the community had grown to number fifteen, leaving only one room spare. Fr Dominic did not lack offers of buildings for new foundations, though few had any real potential. In 1846 a recent convert, William Leigh, offered the Passionists a property at Woodchester in Gloucestershire. This offer, made at the suggestion of Wiseman, was readily accepted. Fr Dominic decided to lead the new community himself and, with a confrere, he secured an old parsonage at Green Forest Village, near Nailsworth, in which to live. This house had the advantage of being very near the site where the new church and monastery were to be built. Leigh was generous, offering to furnish the house himself, but Fr Dominic declined the help writing,

> Do not worry about the furniture. A very few things will suffice for poor monks accustomed to hardships of every sort ... The most essential things will be an altar for the divine Service, and some straw for us to lie on. Other things

such as chairs, tables, books, coals, and the like, will be provided by degrees. The nuns of Mount St Benedict have promised me a set of vestments, and I shall take a chalice and little ciborium with me. The rest will come in time.[221]

Expressing his gratitude to Leigh, Fr Dominic wrote again one week later on 30 March 1846,

We are very comfortable here, even without furniture, except what is quite indispensable. We have a few things for the kitchen, and one table and four chairs lent by Mr. Harrison. Our straw mattresses are now on the floor, but we sleep very well. If, in reality, the iron bedsteads are the poorest of all kinds, I think they will not be against the spirit of our Rule though they are against the letter, for wood is prescribed.[222]

In the meantime, on the feast of the Annunciation, Fr Dominic said the first Mass in the new mission, using a small room in the house. The mission had humble beginnings—on Passion Sunday fifteen people came in the morning and only a handful in the evening—but the fact that the area was deeply non-Conformist, with very few Catholics, appealed to Fr Dominic though he must have guessed that his community would receive a hostile reception as they had experienced at Stone. Still, William Leigh estimated that three hundred attended on Palm Sunday and on Good Friday Fr Dominic preached three times and every time the chapel, which was the largest room in the house, was packed to the door, more people outside, congregating around the windows and the door. Writing to the General, Fr Dominic described how on Palm Sunday he was 'half-suffo-cated by the crowds and the heat, and could hardly go on. A soldier [actually a policeman] was needed to keep order, and the same was true of the Good Friday congregation.' His congregations consisted not only of Catholics but of Protestants who were curious to hear the newcomer to their neighbour-hood, some asking for books on the Catholic faith and a few for instruction. So popular was his preach-ing that Fr Dominic was persuaded to preach at 6 o'clock every evening.

Fr Dominic's trials at Woodchester were not to be as severe as at Stone but there was an underlying hostility. Visiting one house, that of a Mrs Box, a future convert, he found the door slammed in his face by one of her children who had heard in the village school that this was what to do if one of the 'wicked monks' turned up on their doorstep. When her mother heard what had happened the unfortu-nate child was sent to bed without her supper.

Interest in the mission began to grow and invita-tions to found churches in nearby villages came, Fr Dominic reacting to one by writing to the General, saying that 'There is, of course, neither altar, church, nor sign of Christianity in the place, but we must imitate the Apostles and do as best we can, i.e., say Mass where we can, and preach where we can, even in taverns when any kind of a suitable room can be found'.[223] Yet, owing to lack of Passionist priests, he was unable to agree to this or other proposals at this time, having to decline ten offers of new foundations in 1845 alone. Lack of funds, however, did not deter him and by June 1846 Fr Dominic was planning to open a school. 'I shall have to give the teacher—a very good married woman—£25 per annum. I think that she may do much good', he wrote confidently, believing that 'The funds at the disposal of divine Providence are great. Divine Providence will never go bankrupt!'[224] By 1850, when the Passionists transferred the parish into the care of the Dominicans, sixty of the three hundred parishioners at Woodchester were converts.

During these years, at a time when Fr Dominic was away preaching a mission, one of the Passionist students, Confrater Bernard, developed consumption and his life was despaired of. The superior of the house, Fr Vincent Grotti, suggested to the dying man that he approach Fr Dominic and ask him to work a miracle. Years later Fr Bernard recalled,

> I went to his room and as usual found him writing at top speed. When he looked up at me, I asked him to cure me. He replied 'I cannot work miracles.' Then he hesitated for some moments and finally said: 'If it be the will of God'. After that, he made the sign of the Cross on my forehead with his thumb. I thanked him and left his room not knowing whether I was cured or not; all that I can say is that from that moment the thought of dying never again entered my head. Soon afterwards, Fr Dominic announced that he was returning to his work. When he left, we accompanied him to the gate, and as we were going along, he asked me, 'Well, are you going to die?' I answered, 'Father, I

shall not die, but live', to which he added with
great feeling 'And narrate the wonderful works
of God'.[225]

During his eight years in England Fr Dominic
successfully oversaw the establishment of new
Passionist houses at Aston, Woodchester and
Hampstead and procured the land for building a
monastery at Sutton. The foundation stone of the
new church at Aston was laid on 1 March 1846 by
Bishop Walsh, Bishop Wiseman preaching. It was
to cost £1,259 and be opened in 1849. The church
at Woodchester was designed by Charles Hansom,
a previous design by Pugin being rejected due to
its great cost, its foundation stone being laid on
24 November 1846. He was also responsible for
the building of the school-church at Stone cost-
ing £600 and for the opening, on 15 April 1849, of
a temporary chapel at the Hyde, London. As the
inspired but somewhat chaotic Wiseman was usually involved in setting up these foundations it can
be imagined that the finances were not the only
strain on Fr Dominic.

Neither were the organizational demands of
new foundations or buildings his sole concern. He
remained major superior of the Belgian and English
houses thus all decisions of any importance about
the life and work of these houses had to be ultimately
made by him. Every year he made a visitation of the
houses under his purview and undertook a considerable amount of correspondence in respect to all
these responsibilities.

Money was always not a concern for Fr Dominic who was religious in his trust in divine providence, too much so for the General who had to remind him that he and his communities were obliged by the Passionist Rule to beg for alms. Preaching and teaching also continued—it is no wonder that the General pleaded with him to be less relentless in his labours, never succeeding in his requests.

Behind the scenes Fr Dominic also attempted to reconcile quarrels and differences such as the very public spat that was fought through the pages of the press by Lord John Shrewsbury (1791–1852), 16th Earl of Shrewsbury and 16th Earl of Waterford, and the fiery Archbishop of Tuam, John MacHale (1789–1881). Shrewsbury was Lord High Steward of Ireland and had locked horns with the archbishop over the question of Irish nationalism, a quarrel that was aggravated further by personal animosity. Fr Dominic succeeded in quelling their stormy relationship.

In a similar vein, when the editor of the Tablet commenced a series of provocative articles, by private correspondence suggesting more restraint Fr Dominic was able to change the course of the articles to a more constructive path. The sincerity and kindness of his approach, his personal influence, was evident in his day to day being with men and women, whether or not they were Catholic: 'It is said that he was very easy with Protestants who called for him on their death-beds; that he required only true repentance and an act of implicit faith, and then gave them all the Sacraments that they were able to receive'.[226]

Fr Dominic was faithful to living by the resolve that he had made many years before to live by the light of the example of the meekness and gentleness of St Francis de Sales. An example of this would be a mission that he gave with Fr Ignatius Spencer in March 1849 just streets away from Westminster Abbey and Parliament. During the mission Spencer delivered a sermon on the conversion of England that Fr Dominic considered too aggressive in tone. Spencer was upset that he had not the support of his mentor and wondered if Fr Dominic was less enthusiastic in winning England over to the Catholic Church than he had been in the past. Humbly, Fr Dominic agreed that this might be so: a lessening of faith and hope on his part. The next morning, on reflection, Spencer apologized, an apology that was immediately accepted, Fr Dominic saying 'not so much heat, not so much heat, my dear; let us proceed peacefully'.[227]

Whilst the reawakening of the Catholic Church in England offered many opportunities for religious congregations and for the secular clergy, so wide was the field of work with an ever growing Catholic population, the danger of suspicion and jealousy of each other was also present, particularly if funds or vocations were at stake. Fr Dominic never suffered from these diseases. As already mentioned, he made no attempt to win Newman and his disciples for the Passionists despite an acute lack of vocations at the time. Likewise, writing to Spencer before he became a Passionist he reflected on the relationship between secular and religious clergy: 'Let us animate one another to work for God in the common vineyard. The vineyard is large. There is room for all.'[228] It was in this spirit that he sought, and obtained, a close spiritual and working relationship with the Institute of Charity (the Rosminians), Fr Gentili later proposing that Fr Dominic and Fr Ignatius Spencer should become bishops when the English hierarchy was re-established, Fr Dominic being proposed as Bishop of Reading. 'He is in great favour at Oxford', wrote Gentili, 'and he is a learned man and respected by all as a saint and true apostle', the latter thoughts being held by many.[229] This reputation had its more amusing aspects—the future auxiliary bishop of Westminster, Patrick Fenton (1837–1918), recalled an unusual prize offered to his class when he was a boy—the winners would be taken to meet a real live saint. Bishop Fenton wrote,

> I was one of the fortunate boys, and one Saturday we were taken out of London into the countryside where we had lunch. Then we went to see Fr Dominic. He came down to us in the garden and chatted with us in a friendly way, patting us on the head and asking a lot of questions. He noticed, as he was talking, that our own eyes kept straying to the apples in the orchard. He chuckled and went away for a short time, but soon came back with a basketful of apples. He was starting to hand them out when the Brother suggested that we should scram for them. When we started to scram, Fr Dominic was alarmed. The Brother assured him that we would not hurt ourselves and that it was

all in fun, and then he enjoyed it. He brought a second basket of apples and was thoroughly amused as he watched us struggle for them. Before we left, we made him promise to pay a visit to our school. We all agreed that he was a dear old man. He kept his word, and when he came to the school two or three weeks later, he was given a wonderful reception by the boys, who had heard all about him from us.[230]

The image of the chuckling Fr Dominic was one that many were accustomed to seeing—the 'gaiety and affability in the midst of his sanctity' that Newman had noted. Wiseman was to describe him as 'A lion in the might of his intelligence and a child in the simplicity of his heart'.[231] Self-deprecatory humour came naturally to him and, after his death, his confreres remembered him as being humorous in conversation and happy to use his wit in sermons as well, occasionally unintentionally such as when he declared to Birmingham priests that 'No man can be a good priest unless he is a good tinker', the 'th' of thinker not being so easy for him to pronounce.[232] This cheerfulness is all the more remarkable when we remember that interiorly Fr Dominic experienced such spiritual dryness, and exteriorly he was subjected to many a trial too.

25

Trials and Blessings

G IVEN ALL THE DEMANDS upon Fr Dominic's time and his spirit, what he needed most was companions that were as dedicated to the mission as he was. This he was not blessed to have. Fr Amedeus McBride was his first and, for a time, only priest companion in England. From various accounts, he was of little help, refusing to help in the parish and intriguing against Fr Dominic in letters to the bishop and General. McBride returned to Italy the year after Fr Dominic's death, ultimately leaving the order.

Fr Gaudentius Rossi was sent to Fr Dominic shortly after his ordination. In many ways he was the polar opposite of McBride in his activism and youthful zeal to change some of the Passionists' still young traditions. Fr Dominic found this unsettling and worried that Rossi might not be a good influence in forming the Passionist novices. Concerned that Rossi might be appointed his successor, Fr Dominic decided to air his concerns with the General:

> From what I have heard he wants nothing
> less than to change our mode of dress, i.e. the

religious habit, to abandon the midnight office,
to cease the observance of fasts, to abstain from
meat only on Fridays ... in a word, he wants
to make us secular priests, retaining only the
name of Passionists. It is true that he has never
suggested such things to me, but he speaks of
them to others and wants others to talk to me
about them.[233]

Unfortunately, Fr Rossi seems to have not discouraged other Passionists from airing their opinions about Fr Dominic with the General, opinions that Rossi had seeded and let grow in their minds. Thus, Fr Dominic would find himself on the receiving end of critical missives from Rome that were frequently not based in the complex reality of his work in England but rather on the opinion of Rossi. He was living under a cloud. It was out of kindness that some of the young Passionists did not raise areas of concern directly with him but their 'kindness' was more than misplaced. One example of the misunderstanding caused was when Fr Dominic received criticism for 'Italianizing' the English Province—he was scrupulous in doing nothing of the sort but simply strove to preserve the Passionist Rule against Fr Rossi's attempts at innovation.

For this Fr Dominic needed a good novice master to be a positive influence on the new members of the order and so he petitioned the General, proposing the qualities that were needed:

He must be solid, charitable, kind, meek,
placid, and adapted to the English character,
which needs neither fire nor fury, but calmness

and charity ... In England there is no need for haste, the English are enemies of it. Before they make a move they weigh up everything, but once they do move they are steadfast. I very much love this character although it is so different to mine which wants to do everything in the twinkling of an eye. Here I need to curb my hurry. Sometimes, however, my patience gives out.[234]

Another great anguish that Fr Dominic had to bear was how many of the novices that came to the Passionists in England did not persevere or died very young. There were also great blessings, most notably the arrival of the very capable and holy Fr Vincent Grotti in June 1846 and of Fr George Spencer on 21 December of the same year. Fr Dominic had known Spencer since the latter's two years in Rome when he was preparing for priesthood at the English College. Spencer, who was the youngest son of the Second Earl Spencer, one of the most prominent men in English society, had originally been an Anglican priest. He became a Catholic in 1830, being ordained a Catholic priest for the Midlands District in 1832. After ordination he worked in parishes in the Midlands before being sent as a member of staff to Oscott. But Spencer always strove to give more of himself than he felt that the vocation of a secular priest allowed. As he had a generous allowance from the will of his father, he was able and willing to be a generous benefactor to various Catholic projects, including the work of Fr Dominic and the Passionists.

After Newman's conversion, the reception of Spencer into the Passionist order was probably Fr Dominic's second greatest joy. 'He is the noblest and perhaps the man of holiest life of all the priests of this country', Fr Dominic enthused; 'My hopes are that he will be for this branch of our Congregation what St Bernard was for Citeaux, and that he will bring many with him under the standard of the Passion.'[235] 'He is a real saint, in the exact sense of the word', he wrote in another letter, repeating the assertion in other letters.[236]

The 'real saint' was nearly lost in the summer of 1847 when Fr Ignatius became the third victim of the cholera in the retreat at Aston. He, along with the other members of his community, had been tirelessly ministering to the sick and their families of the local area who were suffering from the disease. All three Passionists were to survive, even though two of them were thought to have been at death's door, Spencer being permitted to take temporary vows in case he died. Fr Dominic, however, never succumbed to the illness, despite his great weakness of health. As well as ministering to the sick, he looked for other ways to alleviate the lot of the afflicted. After reading in the *Tablet* of the suffering in the Diocese of Kerry (as it is now called), he organized a collection at Aston and Stone, sending £21 (approximately £2,200 in 2020) to the editor to be forwarded to the bishop. But he wanted to do more, he wanted his community to do something themselves, so he wrote to the editor once more, enclosing four pounds that the community

themselves had scraped together by denying themselves, probably necessary food. With the money he
enclosed a letter that concludes,

> May the Almighty bless this little mustard-
> seed so that it may grow to an amount better
> calculated for the relief of some part of the great
> need now before us. May it stir up those to give
> liberally who have more abundant means of
> doing it. Now is the time for us to show that we
> Catholics are the true followers of Jesus Christ,
> by letting it be seen that we have charity one
> towards another.[237]

Throughout the final years of Fr Dominic's life a particularly painful cross came due to a question of discipline within his order that he believed was integral
to the charism of St Paul of the Cross: extraordinary
as it may now sound, the cross was occasioned by
the burning question of whether or not Passionists in
the new foundations of Belgium and England should
wear sandals. The General and others in Rome main-
tained that the paucity of vocations in these lands
was, in a major part, due to what some deemed was
unsuitable footwear for the colder climes. Fr Dominic not only did not believe that the wearing of sandals was the reason why the Passionists were not
attracting more vocations but also held that if such a
concession were to be granted other penitential elements of the Passionist Rule might also be discarded.
There was considerable strength of opinion on both
sides of the argument, the General writing that

> the adoption of shoes was not a substantial
> change of the Rule, and was required by reason

of the climate and the circumstances. We must either adapt ourselves to these countries or abandon them. St Paul of the Cross who allowed the use of woollen under-vests to offset the cold in Italy would not have insisted on sandals in such harsh climates. Nordic men may admire us for wearing sandals, but they will not imitate us, and unless they imitate us, we cannot establish ourselves. They will not imitate us unless we make our life tolerable as well as mortified. The Stylites made more impression, and caused even greater admiration; but their way of life found no imitators, and their institute (if such it could be called) died when they did.[238]

On the other hand, Fr Dominic believed that the real reasons for the lack of vocations lay in the relative newness of the order and especially in the austerity that was expected of a Passionist:

When we are better known vocations will not be lacking. Let us have authentic Passionists or none. Either let them be as they ought to be, or not be at all. But we shall remain few in numbers! What of it! Who obliges us to be numerous? On the day of judgement, God will not ask how many we were, but only how good we were. But we shall die out in these parts! Let us wait and see. If God sends us good subjects, Deo Gratias. If not, it is preferable to abandon the foundation rather than make it a cemetery, not a nursery, of Passionists.[239]

He was adamant that 'We do more preaching here with bare feet and religious restraint and modesty than with the tongue'.[240] There was a protracted argument concerning the issue, the General becoming increasingly impatient with Fr Dominic's firm resistance to change. Finally, the General, in a harsh letter of reproach, ordered all the religious in Belgium and England to wear shoes, 'beginning with your Paternity', that is, beginning with Fr Dominic himself:

The Pope is of the opinion that shoes should be worn, and has given the necessary faculty; the General and his Consultors, the interpreters of the Rule, have decided that shoes are to be worn; nearly all of my companions are of the same opinion and point to the use of sandals as the reason for our remaining alone and without postulants; (don't be deceived by those who speak differently; they speak like that because they know that it pleases Your Paternity). 'But I who have more insight than the Vicar of Jesus Christ, I who understand the spirit of the Institute better than those whom God has destined to be the guardians and interpreters of the Rule, I who, alone of all those here, understand something of the spirit of God, I think and judge otherwise.' This is, in substance, the attitude taken by Your Paternity, if not explicitly then at least implicitly. And do you judge such sentiments to be in accord with docility, with a lowly opinion of oneself, with humility . . . ? I am sure that your attitude is not dictated by a desire to vindicate your honour by maintaining your opinion, but I am equally sure that you are being deceived by the devil who, misleading you with a semblance of good, knows how to attain his evil ends . . . The devil knows that he will not be heard by Your Paternity unless he presents his suggestions under the cloak of goodness, and so puts forward the maintenance of the Institute, the need to edify, etc. These are exceedingly harmful deceptions because they result in the labourers being few, opportunities being lost and the harvest going, for the greater part, to hell ... Therefore, if we wish for the Conversion of England, we must remove the obstacles to indigenous vocations, and those who neglect to remove such obstacles, while having in their power to do so, are allying themselves with the devil to retard that conversion.

But the sight of us in sandals gives edification ... I believe it, and this is exactly the deception which the devil employs in order to retain his possession of so many souls. The sight of our Venerable Founder without sandals, without hat, without mantle, gave great edification; but when he wanted followers he put on, for the glory of God, both mantle, and hat and sandals. It is not the bare feet alone which give edification, but the coarse habit, poverty of dress, mortification in food, modesty, dignity, reserve, the spirit of God, which are witnessed in one's exterior behaviour. Maintain these things and people will be edified but not alarmed.[241]

The matter was far from over, and it was only after Fr Dominic's death that the General revoked his decision, warning the Passionists of England and Belgium from making any attempt to reduce the efficacious austerity of the order's Rule. Throughout Fr Dominic persisted in following his conscience, responding with due respect for his superiors and ultimately retaining and increasing the affection and esteem that they had for him.

✦ 26 ✦

Final Years

WEAK HEALTH HAD DOGGED FR DOMINIC for decades but by 1847 he sensed that his life was coming to a close. This did not perturb him, as the Oratorian Fr Faber recalled:

> When someone told Fr Dominic, the Passionist, whose memory is dear to so many of us, that she feared the particular judgment, the tears started in his eyes, and he cried out in his natural way, 'Oh, but how sweet to see for the first time the sacred Humanity of Jesus.'[242]

In a letter to a Benedictine nun of November 1848 he encouraged her, writing, 'You must not fear to approach Jesus Christ for He loves you, and we do not fear to approach a person who loves us'.[243]

Despite recurrent physical exhaustion, Fr Dominic gave a mission in Dublin from 29 April to 19 May 1849, accompanied by Frs Spencer and Grotti. 'It gives me great consolation to give this mission with you', he remarked,

> because you can now see for yourselves how Passionist missions ought to be given. I am old, not in years but in infirmities, and soon

I shall be able to give you more effective help
from Heaven than I could on earth; so ask God
to take me.[244]

All three missioners heard confessions for an aver-
age of twelve hours a day and still they were unable
to accommodate all who wanted to confess. People
thronged around Fr Dominic, bowing down to kiss
his hands or a part of his habit, kneeling down to
receive his blessing as he tried to pass. The scene
was similar in other places where he was able to give
missions—in Wapping the crowds tried to prevent
him leaving, settling for accompanying his cab by
walking with it to the railway station five miles away.

He was still writing too, starting work on his final
works, a *Manual of Sacred Eloquence* and *Recollections
Left to Our Young Missionaries in England*, during his
last mission that was given at Drury Lane, London,
21–8 June 1849, completing the writings just two
days before his death. The latter work amounts to
a last testament to the young Passionists advising
them, in a practical and fatherly way, how they
should carry out their ministry.

By the beginning of 1849, Fr Dominic not infre-
quently foretold his coming death: to the Brother
tailor he had to insist that it was not worth making
him a new habit and to close friends he wrote 'I have
finished my course'.[245] But still he drove himself on,
carrying out the prescribed annual visitation to Ere
in August. He clearly told the community that this
was to be the last time that they would see him. The
students of the house, including St Charles of Mount

Argos, insisted on accompanying him to Tournai.
One of them later recalled,

> When we were about a quarter of an hour's
> walk from the town Fr Dominic stopped and
> said: 'My sons, you may go back now. Embrace
> me for one last time in this world. But I hope
> one day to embrace you in heaven!' We insisted
> that he was still young and in good health, and
> that he had no reason to speak like that. 'I tell
> you,' he replied, 'it is the last time. Good-bye.'
> We never saw him again.[246]

How Fr Dominic's earthly life came to its end
is known in great detail thanks to the account of
a fellow Passionist, Fr Louis Pesciaroli.[247] Having
returned from Ere, Fr Dominic spent the night of
Sunday 26 August at Poplar House and is reported
to have been very cheerful at the community recreation that evening. The next day he was setting out
to Woodchester for the opening of the new church
there. Fr Louis asked if he could accompany him as
he had just returned from Australia and he hoped to
meet again Fr Grotti, who was from the same town
as him. Mindful of their vow of poverty, Fr Dominic declined permission to Fr Louis as it was not
necessary for him to go with him, though he added
that should a good reason become known he would
happily change his mind.

The next morning, after a longer than usual time
of preparation for Mass, Fr Dominic told Fr Louis
that he was to accompany him after all but did not
give a reason for his change of mind. As they made

their way to the station Fr Dominic said a number of times that he was soon to die though having heard him say this before, Fr Louis was untroubled by his words.

As their train approached Pangbourne Station, Fr Dominic began to suffer from excruciating pains in his head and, very soon, around his heart and kidneys as well. He told Fr Louis that his time had come. When the train reached Pangbourne Fr Dominic was lifted onto the platform where a doctor, a Mr H. Muggeridge, who happened to be travelling on the train diagnosed that he had suffered a serious heart attack. From the station platform Fr Dominic was carried to a nearby cottage where, after attempting to sit him in a chair, he was laid on straw spread on the brick floor. Writhing in pain and vomiting it was thought by some that he might have fallen victim to the cholera that was then widespread in London. The doctor went around Pangbourne's inns hoping to find somewhere for Fr Dominic to rest more comfortably but the fear of the cholera deterred any from taking him in, 'I will not disturb them for long', Fr Dominic said.

Failing to find refuge in Pangbourne Dr Muggeridge and Fr Louis decided to take Fr Dominic back to Reading and, upon the doctor insisting, Fr Dominic consented. Before leaving Pangbourne Fr Louis heard his confession and again and again Fr Dominic quietly prayed 'Lord, if this is what You desire, Thy will be done', words which Fr Louis referred to as being Fr Dominic's medicine. He was lifted on to the train and laid on straw on the floor of a carriage for the short journey to Reading.

Still in great pain, Fr Dominic was carried off the train, placed in an open carriage and taken to the Railway Tavern where he was put into a bed, the doctor assisting all the while and administering some medicine that gave him a little relief. Dr Muggeridge believed that the patient would recover and, within a few days, be able to resume his journey. After the doctor left Fr Dominic had a half hours' respite from the worst of his suffering but the spasms and convulsions then returned, and he was writhing uncontrollably in agony. He asked Fr Louis to write to Fr Ignatius, then in Holland and ask him to take his place as superior until such a time as the General made other provisions. Fr Louis went into the neighbouring room thinking that Fr Dominic wanted to sleep but Fr Dominic called him back saying 'Do not trust so much in the words of the doctor; in your charity, do not leave me.'

Suddenly at 3 o'clock in the afternoon the spasms worsened, Fr Dominic struggled to breathe and then, stillness. 'I called him', wrote Fr Louis, 'but he made no reply. Then without a moment's delay I gave him Absolution *in articulo mortis*. Dominic's head fell back, and he gave no sign of life. He was dead.'

Having found a doctor who could certify the death Fr Louis began to make the arrangements for Fr Dominic's funeral. First he wrote to the senior priest at Poplar asking him to come to Reading immediately, bringing money to pay for the coffin and the other expenses that were to follow. Fr Dominic had handed him his purse before he died but it contained just a shilling and six pence. As he wrote a maid came into the room to ask if the letter was ready for posting. To Fr Louis's surprise, the maid suddenly knelt, facing the bed where Fr Dominic lay. Fr Louis told her that she could leave the room until the letter was ready. She did so but on her return, she knelt once more. She was not a Catholic, so Fr Louis was curious to know why she did so. She said that she did not quite know herself but simply felt that she *had* to kneel in that room.

That night Fr Louis remained beside Fr Dominic's remains praying through the night. At 4pm the following day the priest arrived from London and Fr Dominic's body was lifted into his coffin. At 6pm they left for London and late the following day the body was transported to Stone, arriving on Thursday 30 August, the funeral being the next day.

When his coffin arrived at Stone it was encased in one of lead before being carried into the little church which Fr Dominic had built where it rested overnight. At 9.30am the Requiem Mass was sung after which Fr Dominic's mortal remains were carried through the streets of Stone, not to the sounds of the insults he had been showered with when first he came to Stone but rather to the sound of sobbing as the procession wound its way through the thousands who had been drawn to Stone for the funeral. The crowds filled the streets, the doorways and windows, even rooftops were used as vantage points as Fr Dominic's remains were bourn to Aston Hall. At Aston the panegyric was delivered by the Rev. John Harkness, chaplain at the nearby Swynnerton Hall and a friend of Fr Dominic: *Pretiosa in conspectus Domini*, he proclaimed, 'Precious in the sight of the Lord is the death of his saints'.[248]

Until 1854 Fr Dominic's body remained buried in a vault before the altar of the new church of St Michael, built by C. F. Hansom. When the Passionists relinquished residence at Aston they transferred the body to their new home of Cotton Hall on 13 January 1855. The relics' time at Cotton was to be short as on 10 November of the same year they were taken to St Anne's Church, Sutton, St Helens, a place that Fr Dominic had prophesied would be his final resting place. But due to the church within which he was buried suffering from mining subsidence, the body of Fr (by then Blessed) Dominic, and the bodies of Ignatius Spencer and Elizabeth (Mother Mary Joseph) Prout were translated to the new church of St Anne and the Blessed Dominic on 30 July 1973. At the opening of the new church on 25 November of that year the Archbishop of Liverpool, the Most Rev'd George Beck, declared, 'We must not anticipate the judgement of the Holy See but it is not altogether fantastic to think that in the future St Anne's may be the shrine of three saints intimately associated with the development of Catholic life in this country during the past 150 years'.

The cause for the canonization of Fr Dominic was commenced in 1889 and he was beatified by Pope St

Paul VI on 27 October 1963, during the convocation of the Second Vatican Council and in the presence of Hector Chianura, the man who had been miraculously cured of a terminal lung condition through the intercession of Blessed Dominic. Fifty years later, preaching in the church wherein Blessed Dominic is buried, Archbishop Bernard Longley noted

> It is no coincidence that Blessed Dominic of the Mother of God was beatified 50 years ago during that [the Second Vatican] Council. One of the central themes of the Council was that the Church should come to understand afresh the world in which she is called to witness to Christ—so that we can find new and effective ways to preach the good news, so that we can understand what it is that people hear when we preach the Gospel, so that we can find ways of touching their hearts by our Christian witness.

The witness of Blessed Dominic was to the overwhelming love of Christ in His Passion and this was for him a transforming power. This experience transfigured his life and urged him to joyfully take his part in drawing together 'the scattered children of God', above all through his ministry in England. Blessed Dominic's very life was the sermon that touched hearts and opened minds to hear the Gospel of Jesus Christ afresh, a sermon that moved many to find peace and the light of truth.

Blessed Dominic of the Mother of God—pray for us.

Prayer

O God, who so lovingly raised Blessed Dominic to the heights of holiness, learning and apostolic zeal and made him a powerful minister of your mercy, listen to our humble request.

We pray that you will in your goodness, grant a miracle through the intercession of Blessed Dominic, so that the Church may further honour him on earth and that many more people will come to know and invoke the help of this faithful servant of the Church.

We ask this through Christ Our Lord. Amen.

Blessed Dominic Barberi: Pray for us.

Please report favours granted through the intercession of Blessed Dominic to

Fr Ben Lodge CP,
Passionist Retreat Centre,
Minsteracres,
Consett,
Co. Durham,
DH8 9RT

ABBREVIATIONS

A   *Autobiography. Traccia della divina misericordia per la conversion di un peccatore, Dominic of the Mother of God, Brescia, 1959.*

ABC   Archives of the Benedictines, Colwich.

AG   General Archives of the Passionists, Rome.

AP   Archives of the Postulator General of the Passionists

AW   Wilson, A, *Blessed Dominic Barberi—Supernaturalized Briton,* London, 1967.

CA, CC, AB etc. Biographical documents about Blessed Dominic in AP. If followed by a name indicates manuscripts of other men about Dominic.

D   *Life of the Very Rev. Fr. Dominic of the Mother of God,* Pius Devine CP, London, 1898.

DD   Spiritual Diary of Fr Dominic, ed. Conrad Charles, Provincial Archives.

F   *Il Beato Domenico della Madre di Dio,* P. Federico dell'Addolorata, CP.

LD   Newman, J.H., *The Letters and Diaries of John Henry Newman,* ed. C. Dessain, T. Gornall, I. Ker, *et al.,* 32 vols, Oxford, 1978–2008.

MSS   Manuscripts of Blessed Dominic in AP.

P   *Life of the Servant of God P. Domenico,* P. Filippo della SS. Annunziata, Tipografia Bono, Ferentino, 1860.

Pos.   Positio super virtutibus, Summarium, 1933.

RM   *Recollections left to Our Young Missionaries,* B. Dominic, in Provincial Archives.

SGC   Archives of St Gabriel's Retreat, Ormskirk.

U   Young, U., *The Life and Letters of the Venerable Dominic (Barberi) C.P., Founder of the Passionists in Belgium and England,* London, 1926.

Y   Young, U., *Dominic Barberi in England,* London, 1935.

Notes

[1] *Il Celeste Pedagogo*, dialogue 6.
[2] A, 17.
[3] CC, 37. P. Luigi di S. Anna.
[4] A, 16.
[5] *AP Bir.* 180.
[6] *Excellence de Marie*, Tournai, 1899, 6.
[7] GC, 35 and 130.
[8] A, 20.
[9] A, 21–2.
[10] *Ibid.* 22.
[11] CC Fonti Vive, I, 131.
[12] A, 23.
[13] A, 51.
[14] A, 52.
[15] AW, 25.
[16] A, 52.
[17] *Ibid.*
[18] A, 56
[19] AV, 79–80; Y, 3–4
[20] A, 57–8.
[21] A, 82–3; Y, 5–6.
[22] Pos., 124; CDO, 7–8.
[23] A, 74–5.
[24] Pos., 172.
[25] AG, *Proc. Ord. Rom.*, AII, 1, 288.
[26] AW, 50.
[27] P, 35.
[28] DD, 44.
[29] AW, 54.
[30] P, 34–5.
[31] DD, 63.
[32] AW, 56.
[33] DD, 61–2.
[34] MSS V, 3, 45 seq. P, 36–8. *Il Celeste Pedagogo*, dial. XV.
[35] *Ibid.*
[36] *Ibid.*
[37] DD, 47.

38 *Ibid.*
39 *Ibid.*
40 AG, *Summ.,* 441, 446.
41 CB, 22 and AG *Proc. Birm.,* 158.
42 AP, *Dialogue on Prayer,* 35.
43 AW, 65.
44 AP, *Il Gemito Della Colomba,* 146.
45 *Ibid.* 147.
46 *Ibid.* VI, p. 151
47 AW, 66.
48 DD, 34–5.
49 DD, 57–8.
50 AW, 67.
51 AG, *Ap., Birm.,* 158.
52 AP, *Il Gemito Della Colomba,* V.
53 AG, *Proc. Birm.,* 158.
54 DD, 7.
55 DD, 9.
56 DD, 50–4.
57 DD, 2.
58 *Ibid.*
59 DD, 4.
60 DD, 31.
61 DD, 56.
62 MSS VI, 21, 221–2.
63 P, 39.
64 MSS VII, I, 221.
65 AG, *Platea di S. Angelo,* 55–6; AG, *Birm. App.,* 46.
66 DD, 70.
67 AG, *Proc. Rom.,* 17, 67.
68 DD, 69–70.
69 DD, 78.
70 CD, 53.
71 DD, 73.
72 D. Barberi, *Apparato all'Apostolico Ministero,* 18.
73 *Ibid.* 108.
74 MSS XII, 13.
75 DD, P, 32.
76 DD, 64.
77 P, 41.
78 CB, 22, D; P Felice.
79 P, 42.

80 P, 43.
81 DD, 72.
82 A, 15–15.
83 AW, 93.
84 AP, *Apparato all'Apostolico Ministro*, 72, 77.
85 *Ibid*. 79.
86 RM, 31.
87 CB, 22 D-P Felice.
88 AP, *Fonte Vive*, 1959, 486–9, 493. Also MSS VI, 17: *Esercizi a Monache*, 165–70.
89 AW, 108.
90 MSS VII, 1, 230.
91 CBC.
92 EX, X–XI.
93 DD, 59–60.
94 P, 74.
95 AG, *Proc. Birm.* 51; MSS IV, 9; also *Proc. Tour.*, 167–8.
96 Y, 6.
97 *Il Gemito*, V.
98 Cf. AG, *Ap., Vit.*, 293; *Platea*, Sept. 1832.
99 CA, I, P Agostino.
100 U, 58.
101 AW, 129–30.
102 AW, 102.
103 CB, 32—P Giustino.
104 F, 162.
105 AG, Summ 25, 27.
106 Pope St Paul VI, address on the beatification of Blessed Dominic, *Acta Apost. Sedis* 55 (1963), 1020–1.
107 AW, 133.
108 AW, 134–5.
109 DD, 95.
110 DD, 96–7.
111 AW, 143; Cf. extracts from the conventual books of the Passionist Congregation. Gen. Archives, Rome.
112 Brother Seraphim AG, *Proc. Ord. Par.* 310.
113 AG, *Proc. Ord. Rom.* 1, 128.
114 DD, 86.
115 P, 88.
116 P, 181; *Proc. Ord. Fer.* 27; *Diario Necrologico*—P Eustachio, 441.
117 OV, 174, 307–8.
118 OV, 209–11.

[119] AW, 167–8.

[120] AW, 169.

[121] OV, 61, 143.

[122] Outlines of examens, MSS VI, 5, 191–2.

[123] MSS XIII, 68.

[124] AP, *Apparato all'Apostolico Ministero*, 83.

[125] *Ibid.*, 77.

[126] *Ibid.*, 75–6.

[127] *Ibid.*, 60–3.

[128] AP, Mariaology I, 23.

[129] Letters Testa/Barberi. AG Y, 16.

[130] AG, *Proc. Ord. Rom.*, 80–1.

[131] *Ibid.*, 88–9.

[132] CD, 65 — P Ambrogio M del B Gesu.

[133] AG, Correspondence Testa Barberi 12 June.

[134] Y, 221.

[135] AG, VI.

[136] U, 171. S; Pos., 223–5.

[137] Arcana Verba in Autobiography, 84 ss; Y, 7–8.

[138] Conrad II, 210–11, etc., Correspondence, AG, VI; Y, 56–7.

[139] AG; F, 307–9.

[140] Y, 66.

[141] AW, 230.

[142] D, 181–2.

[143] Letter from George Spencer to Mrs Canning, 24 February 1841, ABC.

[144] AW, 234.

[145] Pius a Sp. Sancto, *Life of Father Ignatius of St Paul, Passionist (The Hon. and Rev. George Spencer). Compiled chiefly from his Autobiography, Journal, and Letters*, Dublin, 1866, 278.

[146] MSS XIX.

[147] AG, Prov. S. Michele, fondo Belgio.

[148] Y, 71.

[149] Y, 75.

[150] MSS IV, 11, 1.

[151] Fr Bernard O'Loughlin: Archiv. Ormskirk.

[152] AP, MSS IV, 11, 5–17.

[153] Fr Bernard O'Loughlin: Archiv. Ormskirk.

[154] AW, 244.

[155] SGC Barberi Letters no. IX Conrad II, 248–9.

[156] Y, 83–4.

[157] Pos., 679.

[158] Pos., 687.

159 U, 213.
160 U, 213.
161 Y, 99.
162 M. Hearney: AG, *Proc. Birm.*, 69.
163 Proc. Paris. Copy. AG, 311.
164 Fr Bernard O'Loughlin, AP, 363.
165 AG, *Proc. Birm.* 59.
166 D, 158–60.
167 F, 347–8.
168 DD, 7.
169 DD, 66.
170 U, 227–8.
171 RM, 31.
172 RM, 30.
173 MSS VI, 21, 37.
174 AW, 274.
175 AW, 275.
176 *Lettere*, 9 February 1831, Y, 10–12.
177 AW, 291.
178 The complete text of Fr Dominic's letter can be found in D and U.
179 Archives, Ormskirk.
180 Letter to the General 10 October 1841, Archives, Ormskirk.
181 MSS IV, 11, 581–6; Supplement, 353–8.
182 Y, 214–5.
183 Cf. AW, 295.
184 *LD 8*, Newman to Bloxam, 23 February 1841, 42.
185 AW, 297.
186 Y, 216.
187 Y, 102.
188 Y, 219–20.
189 Y, 220–1.
190 Y, 223–4.
191 U, 255–6.
192 Y, 136.
193 *LD 10*, Newman to Mrs Bowden, 3 October 1845, 772.
194 Archiv. Ormskirk.
195 *Ibid*.
196 AW 302.
197 *LD 10*, Newman to Richard Stanton, 4 October 1845, 777.
198 *LD 11*, Newman to Henry Wilberforce, 7 October 1845, 3.
199 *LD 11*, Newman to Mrs William Froude, 7 October 1845, 7.
200 *LD 11*, Newman to Mrs J. W. Bowden, 8 October 1845, 5.

201 *LD 11*, Newman to Henry Wilberforce, 7 October 1845, 3.

202 *LD 11*, Newman to Mrs Bowden, 8 October 1845, 5.

203 *LD 11*, Newman to R. W. Church, 8 October 1845, 6.

204 *LD 11*, Newman to Isaac Williams, 8 October 1845, 10.

205 AW, 305.

206 *LD 30*, Newman to Cardinal Parochi, 2 October 1889, 276.

207 AW, 308.

208 Part III, Chapter 10.

209 Y, 138–9.

210 Original in archives of Birmingham Oratory.

211 Y, 149.

212 Archiv. Ormskirk.

213 *LD 13*, Newman to A. J. Hanmer, 16 January 1850, 389.

214 *LD 11*, Newman to Henry Wilberforce, 26 February 1845, 129.

215 *LD 11*, Newman to James Hope, 23 December 1845, 76.

216 *LD 11*, Newman to J. D. Dalgairns, 10 December 1845, 56.

217 AW, 314.

218 J. H. Newman, 'The Second Spring', in *Sermons Preached on Various Occasions*, London, 1908, 176.

219 B. Camm, *Ven. Dominic Barberi and the Conversion of England*, London, 1922.

220 Pope St Paul VI, address on the beatification of Blessed Dominic, *Acta Apost. Sedis* 55 (1963), 1024.

221 U, 272–3.

222 U, 274.

223 Y, 161.

224 Y, 161–2.

225 A G, *Proc. Ord. Paris*, 330; *AG Birm.*, 32, 37.

226 D, 211.

227 CC, 33.

228 U, 165–7.

229 AW, 327.

230 AG, *Proc. Birm.*, 43.

231 AW, 350.

232 AW, 345.

233 AG, B/T 13 December 1848.

234 AG, B/T 1844, 13 November.

235 Y, 165–6, 169.

236 AW, 340.

237 U, 286–7.

238 AG, T/B, 9 June 1842.

239 AW, 352.

Notes

240 AW, 352–3.
241 AG, T/B, 6 January 1847.
242 F. Faber, *All for Jesus*, London, 1853, 307.
243 Letter 10 November 1848—original in Benedictine Convent, Colwich.
244 Record of Missions and Retreats, Aston Hall, 10. Also RM, 39–44.
245 CD, 68, 4, 24; CDO, 34; *Proc. Ord. Tourn.*, 168. And Pos., 245; Y, 205.
246 AP, *Proc. Ord. Tourn.*, 74.
247 AP, Letter to the General, August 1849; P, 155–60.
248 Y, 335.

BIBLIOGRAPHY

Camm, B., *Ven. Dominic Barberi and the Conversion of England*, London, 1922.

Faber, F., *All for Jesus*, London, 1853.

Fothergill, B., *Nicholas Wiseman*, London, 1963.

Gwyn, D., *Cardinal Wiseman*, Dublin, 1950.

—— *Father Luigi Gentili and his Mission (1801–1848)*, Dublin, 1951.

—— *A Hundred Years of Catholic Emancipation (1829–1929)*, London, 1929.

Gwynn, D., *Father Dominic Barberi*, London, 1947.

Hamer, D. S., *Sr Elizabeth Prout*, London, 2009.

Ker, J., *John Henry Newman. A Biography*, Oxford, 1988.

Lodge, B., *Dominic Barberi*, London, 2008.

—— *Ignatius Spencer*, London, 2005.

Newman, J. H., *Apologia pro Vita Sua*, The two versions of 1864 and 1865 preceded by Newman's and Kingsley's Pamphlets. With an Introduction by W. Ward, Oxford 1913.

Newman, J. H., *Sermons Preached on Various Occasions*, London, 1908.

—— *The Letters and Diaries of John Henry Newman*, ed. C. Dessain, T. Gornall, I. Ker, *et al.*, 32 vols, Oxford, 1978-2008.

Pius a Sp. Sancto, *Life of Father Ignatius of St Paul, Passionist (The Hon. & Rev. George Spencer). Compiled chiefly from his Autobiography, Journal, & Letters*, Dublin, 1866.

—— *Life of the Very Rev. Father Dominic of the Mother of God (Barberi), Passionist, Founder of the Congregation of the Passion or Passionists in Belgium and England*, London, 1898.

Purcell, E. S., *Life and Letters of Ambrose Phillipps de Lisle*. Ed. E. de Lisle, London, 1900.

Schiefen, R. J., *Nicholas Wiseman and the Transformation of English Catholicism*, Shepherdstown, 1984.

Schofield, N., and G. Skinner, *The English Cardinals*, Oxford, 2007.

—— *The English Vicars Apostolic*, Oxford, 2009.

Skinner, G., *Father Ignatius Spencer—English Noble and Christian Saint*, Leominster, 2018.

Van den Busssche, J., *Ignatius (George) Spencer Passionist (1799–1864) – Crusader of Prayer for England and Pioneer of Ecumenical Prayer*, Leuven, 1991.

Vereb, J., *Ignatius Spencer—Apostle of Christian Unity*, London, 1992.

Dominic Barberi

Ward, B., *The Sequel to Catholic Emancipation 1830–1850: The Story of the English Catholics continued down to the Establishment of their Hierarchy in 1850*, London, 1915.

Ward, W., *The Life and Times of Cardinal Wiseman*, vols. 1 and 2, London, 1898.

Wilson, A, *Blessed Dominic Barberi—Supernaturalized Briton*, London, 1967.

Young, U., *The Life and Letters of the Venerable Dominic (Barberi) C.P., Founder of the Passionists in Belgium and England*, London, 1926.

Milton Keynes UK
Ingram Content Group UK Ltd.
UKHW011450310723
426082UK00001B/39

9 780852 449776